From Demo to Free

to

CrimethInc. ex-Workers' Collective ♥ 2017 ♦ Salem, Oregon

cracy

The difference between government and self-determination

This book is the result of years of dialogue between participants in social movements spanning three continents. All but one of the authors have chosen to retain their anonymity in order to emphasize the collective nature of the project.

N©!2017 CrimethInc. ex-Workers' Collective

CrimethInc. Far East
PO Box 4671
Salem OR 97302
inquiries@crimethinc.com

You can obtain a great deal of related material via
www.crimethinc.com

Printed in Canada by unionized printers
on 100% post-consumer recycled paper

FROM
DEMOCRACY
TO
FREEDOM

Democracy is the most universal political ideal of our day. George Bush invoked it to justify invading Iraq; Obama congratulated the rebels of Tahrir Square for bringing it to Egypt; Occupy Wall Street claimed to have distilled its pure form. From the Democratic People's Republic of North Korea to the autonomous region of Rojava, practically every government and popular movement calls itself democratic.

And when there are problems with democracy, what's the cure? Everyone agrees: *more democracy.* Since the turn of the century, we've seen a spate of new movements promising to deliver *real* democracy, in contrast to ostensibly democratic institutions that they describe as exclusive, coercive, and alienating.

Is there a common thread that links all these different kinds of democracy? Which of them is the *real* one? Can any of them deliver the inclusivity and freedom we associate with the word?

Impelled by our own experiences in directly democratic movements, we've returned to these questions. Our conclusion is that the dramatic imbalances in economic and political power that inspired occupations and uprisings from New York City to Sarajevo are not incidental defects in specific democracies, but structural features that date back to the origins of democracy itself; they appear in practically every example of democratic government through the ages. Representative democracy preserved all the bureaucratic apparatus that was originally invented to serve kings; direct democracy tends to recreate this on a smaller scale, even outside the formal structures of the state. *Democracy is not the same as self-determination.*

To be sure, many good things are regularly described as democratic. This is not an argument against discussions, collectives, assemblies, networks, federations, or working with people you don't always agree with. The argument, rather, is that when we engage in those practices, if we understand what we are doing as *democracy*—as a form of participatory government rather than a collective pursuit of freedom—then sooner or later, we will recreate all the problems associated with less democratic forms of government. This goes for rep-

resentative democracy and direct democracy alike, and even for consensus process.

Rather than championing democratic procedures as an end in themselves, let's evaluate them according to the values that drew us to democracy in the first place: egalitarianism, inclusivity, the idea that each person should control her own destiny. If democracy is not the most effective way to actualize them, what is?

As fiercer and fiercer struggles rock today's democracies, the stakes of this discussion keep getting higher. If we go on trying to replace the prevailing order with a more participatory version of the same thing, we'll keep ending up right back where we started, and others who share our disillusionment will gravitate towards more authoritarian alternatives. We need a framework that can fulfill the promises democracy has betrayed.

What Is Democracy?

What is democracy, exactly? Most of the textbook defini-
tions have to do with majority rule or government by elected
representatives. Yet the word is often used more broadly to
invoke self-determination and equality as abstract ideals; a
few radicals* have gone so far as to argue that *real* democracy
only takes place outside and against the state's monopoly on
power. Is democracy a means of state government, a form of
horizontal self-organization, or something else?

Let's begin by distinguishing two distinct usages of the
term. Used precisely, democracy denotes a specific set of
decision-making practices with a history extending back to
ancient Greece. By association, the word invokes an abstract
aspiration to egalitarian, inclusive, and participatory politics.
The fundamental question for those who embrace these aspirations is whether the practices associated with democracy are
the most effective way to realize them.

The range of procedures associated with democracy is wide
indeed: it includes everything from the Electoral College to
informal consensus process. All of these are ways to legitimize
a power structure as representing the participants. What else
do they have in common?

We can look for clues in the origins of the term itself. The
word democracy derives from the ancient Greek *dēmokratía,* from
dêmos "people" and *krátos* "power." In short, democracy is *rule
by the people.* We see the same formulation in contemporary
Latin American social movements: *poder popular.*

But which people? And what sort of power?

These root words, *demos* and *kratos,* suggest two common
denominators of all democratic procedures: a way of determining who participates in the decision-making and a way of
enforcing decisions. In short, citizenship and policing. These

---

* For example, Cindy Milstein, in *Democracy Is Direct*: "Direct democracy . . . is completely at odds with both the state and capitalism."

are the essentials of democracy; they are what make it a form of government. Anything short of that is more properly described as *anarchy*—the absence of government, from the Greek *an-* "without" and *arkhos* "ruler."

Who qualifies as *demos,** the people? For there to be legitimate decisions, there have to be defined conditions of legitimacy and a specific set of people who meet them.† Consequently, every form of democracy requires a way of distinguishing between included and excluded. This dividing line could be status in a legislature, citizenship in a nation, membership in a group, or participation in neighborhood assemblies; it could be race, gender, property ownership, age, or legal status. Who gets to make the decisions might simply be determined by who can show up to meetings—but even in the most informal cases, democratic structures always require a mechanism of inclusion and exclusion.

In this regard, democracy institutionalizes the provincial, chauvinist character of its Greek origins at the same time as it seemingly offers a model that could involve all the world. This is why it has proven so compatible with nationalism and the state; democracy presupposes the Other, who is not accorded the same rights or political agency.

The division between included and excluded was articulated clearly enough at the dawn of modern democracy in Rousseau's influential text *Of the Social Contract,* in which he asserts that there is no contradiction between democracy and slavery. The more "evildoers" are in chains, he suggests, the more perfect the freedom of the citizens. This zero-sum conception of freedom is foundational to democracy—hence the incentive to gatekeeping.

Now let's turn to the other root, *kratos.* Democracy shares this suffix with aristocracy, autocracy, bureaucracy, plutocracy,

---

* Some argue that etymologically, *demos* never meant *all* people, but only particular social classes. See, for example, *Contra la Democracia,* published in Spain by the Coordination of Anarchist Groups.

† Cf. Sarah Song, "The Boundary Problem in Democratic Theory: Why the Demos Should Be Bounded by the State."

"There is no contradiction between exercising democracy and legitimate central administrative control according to the well-known balance between centralization and democracy ... Democracy consolidates relations among people, and its main strength is respect. The strength that stems from democracy assumes a higher degree of adherence in carrying out orders with great accuracy and zeal."

– Saddam Hussein, "Democracy: A Source of Strength for the Individual and Society"

and technocracy. Each of these terms describes government by some subset of society, but they all share a common logic. That common thread is *kratos,* power.

What kind of power? Let's consult the ancient Greeks once more.

In classical Greece, every abstract concept was personified by a divine being. Kratos was an implacable Titan embodying the kind of coercive force associated with state power. One of the oldest sources in which Kratos appears is the play *Prometheus Bound,* composed by Aeschylus in the early days of Athenian democracy. The play opens with Kratos forcibly escorting the

2500 YEARS AGO
WE DECLARED **WAR** ON THE **WORLD!**

WE CALL THIS WAR
DEMOCRACY!

shackled Prometheus, who is being punished for stealing fire from the gods to give to humanity. Kratos appears as a jailer unthinkingly carrying out Zeus's orders—a brute "made for any tyrant's acts."[*]

The sort of force personified by Kratos is what democracy has in common with autocracy and every other form of rule. They share the institutions of coercion: the legal apparatus, the police, and the military, all of which preceded democracy and have repeatedly outlived it. These are the tools "made for any tyrant's acts," whether the tyrant at the helm is a king, a class of bureaucrats, or "the people" themselves. "Democracy means simply the bludgeoning of the people by the people for the people," as Oscar Wilde put it. Mu'ammer al Gaddafi echoed this approvingly a century later in *The Green Book,* without irony: *"Democracy is the supervision of the people by the people."*

In modern-day Greek, *kratos* is simply the word for state. To understand democracy, we have to look closer at government itself.

Monopolizing Legitimacy

"As in absolute governments the King is law, so in free countries the law ought to be King."

— Thomas Paine, *Common Sense*

As a form of government, democracy serves to produce a single order out of a cacophony of desires, absorbing the resources and activities of the minority into policies dictated by the majority.

In order to accomplish this, every democracy requires a space of legitimate decision-making distinct from the rest of life. This could be a congress in a parliament building, or

[*] Thomas Medwin's translation.

> "Can there not be a government
> in which majorities do not
> virtually decide right and wrong,
> but conscience?"

> – Henry David Thoreau, *Civil Disobedience*

a general assembly on a sidewalk, or an app soliciting votes via iPhone. In every case, the ultimate source of legitimacy is not the immediate needs and desires of the participants, but a particular decision-making process and protocol. In a state, this is called "the rule of law," though the principle does not necessarily require a formal legal system.

This is the essence of government: decisions made in one space determine what can take place in all other spaces. The result is alienation—the friction between what is decided and what is lived.

Democracy promises to solve the problem of alienation by incorporating everyone into the space of decision-making: the rule of all by all. "The citizens of a democracy submit to the law because they recognize that, however indirectly, they are submitting to themselves as makers of the law."* But if all those decisions were actually made by the people they impact, there would be no need for a means of enforcing them.

How much do you buy into the idea that the democratic process should trump your own conscience and values? Let's try a quick exercise. Imagine yourself in a democratic republic with slaves—say, ancient Athens, or ancient Rome, or the United States of America until the end of 1865. Would you

* http://www.ait.org.tw/infousa/zhtw/DOCS/whatsdem/whatdm4.htm, a site produced and maintaine d by the US Department of State's Bureau of International Information Programs.

obey the law and treat people as property while endeavoring to change the laws, knowing full well that whole generations might live and die in chains in the meantime? Or would you act according to your conscience in defiance of the law, like Harriet Tubman and John Brown?

If you would follow in the footsteps of Harriet Tubman, then you, too, believe that there is something more important than the rule of law. This is a problem for anyone who wants to make conformity with the law or with the will of the majority into the final arbiter of legitimacy.

THIS IS A DEMOCRACY NOT AN ANARCHY.
WE HAVE A SYSTEM IN THE COUNTRY TO
CHANGE RULES. WHEN YOU ARE ON THE
SUPREME COURT, YOU CAN MAKE THAT
DECISION.

- ROBERT STUTMAN

Checks and Balances

What protects the minorities in a winner-take-all system? Advocates of democracy explain that minorities will be protected by institutional provisions—by *checks and balances.*

In other words, the same structure that holds power over them is supposed to protect them from itself. There is no other pill to take, so swallow the one that made you ill.

This seeming paradox didn't trouble the framers of the US Constitution because the minority whose rights they were chiefly concerned with protecting was the class of property owners—which already had disproportionate leverage on state institutions. As James Madison put it in 1787,

> Our government ought to secure the permanent interests of the country against innovation. Landholders ought to have a share in the government, to support these invaluable interests, and to balance and check the other. They ought to be so constituted as to protect the minority of the opulent against the majority.

So the institutions of majority rule may indeed serve to protect minorities—if we are talking about the *most privileged* minorities. Otherwise, it's just naïve.

Trusting that institutional provisions can serve to hold majorities in check means gambling that institutions will always be better than the people who operate them. In fact, the more power we vest in the instruments of government, the more dangerous those instruments will be when they are turned against the marginalized. If the object is to protect minorities from majorities, centralizing all power and legitimacy in a single institutional structure can only exacerbate the problem.

Minorities must have the power to defend themselves if they are not to be dominated by majorities. Only a decentralized distribution of power reinforced by a collective commitment to solidarity can ensure that they will always be able to do so.

> "The great difficulty lies in this: you must first enable the government to control the governed; and in the next place oblige it to control itself."
>
> – James Madison, *The Federalist*

Rather than everyone uniting to impose majority rule, then, every partisan of freedom should cooperate to prevent the possibility of rule itself. This cannot be a merely institutional project; it must transcend any particular set of institutions, lest their limitations become its own.

The idea that democratic institutions could protect the rights of individuals serves to justify state power at the expense of personal freedom.* The implication is that, in order to preserve a certain degree of conditional freedom for individuals, government must possess ultimate authority—the capacity to take freedom away from everyone. Using the pretext that, as Isaiah Berlin put it, "Freedom for the wolf is death for the lamb," the state seeks to produce sheep, reserving the position of wolf for itself.

But instead of thinking of liberty as a zero-sum game to be regulated by the state, what if we imagine it as something cumulative? Where others accept tyranny, we must live under it as well; but when they stand up to it, they create opportunities for us to do the same. If we understand freedom as a collectively produced relationship to our potential rather than a static bubble of private rights, being free is not simply a question of being protected by the authorities, but the project of creating open-ended spaces of possibility. In that view, the freedom of one person adds to the freedom of all,† whereas the more that coercive force is centralized, the less freedom there is for anyone.

---

* See Walter E. Williams, "Democracy or a Republic."

† "I am truly free only when all human beings, men and women, are equally free. The freedom of others, far from negating or limiting my freedom, is, on the contrary, its necessary premise and confirmation." –Mikhail Bakunin

The Consent of the Governed

"Only the present, truly assembled people
are the people and produce the public...
Rousseau's famous thesis that the people
cannot be represented* rests on this truth.
They cannot be represented, because they
must be present, and only something absent,
not something present, can be represented. As
a present, genuinely assembled people, they
exist in the pure democracy with the greatest
possible degree of identity."

– Carl Schmitt,[†] *Constitutional Theory*

Article 21 of the United Nations' 1948 Universal Declaration of
Human Rights states that "The will of the people shall be the
basis of the authority of government." Governments derive
their legitimacy "from the consent of the governed," reads
the Declaration of Independence. But how do we determine
whether the governed have given their consent?

* "The instant a people gives itself representatives, it ceases to be
free." – Jean-Jacques Rousseau, Of the Social Contract

† Movements that emphasize physical presence in public space, such
as Occupy Wall Street, share this priority with Nazis like Carl Schmitt,
chief jurist of Hitler's regime in Germany. This is the oldest form of
democracy—Spartan rather than Athenian—in which the masses
legitimize a movement or ruling party as *representative* by acclaiming
it in person, rather than through elections.

Let's start with the most egregious cases. Today well over a billion people live in explicitly authoritarian regimes that nonetheless proclaim themselves democratic. We can begin by identifying what common denominators these self-described democracies share with governments like the one that prevails in the United States.

In a sense, there can be no government without the participation of the governed; no *kratos* without the *demos*.‡ Hence, at one end of the spectrum of purported democracies, we find regimes like the People's Republic of China—which Mao, taking after Lenin,§ christened *"the people's democratic dictatorship."*¶

If democracy is just a form of popular government through representatives, these three words do not necessarily contradict each other. Winning an election is one way to claim the legitimacy of having been chosen by the people; being acclaimed in the streets or instituted by popular violence are other ways. In ancient Sparta, leaders were elected to the council of elders by a shouting contest—the candidate who received the loudest applause won.** The technical term for this is *acclamation*. The democratic governments that first took power in the French revolutions of 1848 and 1870 were chosen in much the same way: revolutionaries proposed lists of representatives to the assembled masses from the windows

‡ In *Discipline and Punish* and other works, Foucault makes a compelling argument to this effect, underscoring how people on all levels of society contribute to perpetuating hierarchies.

§ For example, in "The Revolutionary-Democratic Dictatorship of the Proletariat and the Peasantry." Two generations later, children who grew up in the USSR were taught that the world was divided into two zones: the *democratic* countries (the ones under Soviet rule or influence) and the *imperialist* countries (in the sphere of US influence).

¶ "The right to vote belongs only to the people, not to the reactionaries. The combination of these two aspects, democracy for the people and dictatorship over the reactionaries, is the people's democratic dictatorship." – Mao Tse-tung, "On the People's Democratic Dictatorship"

** See, for example, "Shouts, Murmurs, and Votes: Acclamation and Aggregation in Ancient Greece," by Melissa Schwartzberg.

of the Hôtel de Ville, to gauge the popular reaction. In 2015, in Macedonia, the government and the opposition called rival demonstrations, each striving to validate its claim to power by mobilizing more people—election by rally rather than ballot. If, like Barack Obama, we consider the Egyptian revolution of 2011 *democratic*,* we too are validating participatory violence as a means of legitimizing governments.

And if people may choose a government by shouting or popular violence, it is not much of a stretch to imagine that they might choose a government by *doing nothing*, too. Many a dictator has been paraded before the people to the same *acclamation* that elected politicians in Sparta and Paris. Wouldn't the inhabitants of the Democratic People's Republic of North Korea have shaken off Kim Jong-il if they wished to? And if we grant that they did not because they could not, what does that tell us about those who consent to government in "real" democracies like the United States? Perhaps, regardless of whether they may vote in elections, they accept the imposition of law only because they are not able to defend themselves against the most powerful military in the history of the solar system. Do we choose the governments that rule us because we want them, or do we want them because we have no other choice?

This is a problem if you consider governments to derive their legitimacy from the consent of the governed. For that claim to hold water, it must be easy enough to topple the entire apparatus of the state that any majority might do it without great inconvenience. Real freedom is not just a question of how much participation we are offered *within* a given structure, but of how freely we may change it.

---

* See "Remarks by the President on Egypt," February 11, 2011. One might object that the American, French, and Egyptian revolutions are considered "democratic" not because they represented the people choosing a new form of government, but because they set up the conditions for elections to be properly conducted. Yet we are still in the habit of regarding these revolutions as representing "the will of the people" in some form—or else whence comes the legitimacy of the electoral processes they instituted?

The Original Democracy

"Are we supposed to believe that before the Athenians, it never really occurred to anyone, anywhere, to gather all the members of their community in order to make joint decisions in a way that gave everyone equal say?"

-David Graeber,
Fragments of an Anarchist Anthropology

In ancient Athens, the much-touted "birthplace of democracy," we already see the exclusion and coercion that have been essential features of democratic government ever since.† Only adult male citizens with military training could vote; women, slaves, debtors, and all who lacked Athenian blood were excluded. At the very most, democracy involved less than a fifth of the population.

Indeed, slavery was more prevalent in ancient Athens than in other Greek city states, and women had fewer rights relative to men. Greater equality among male citizens apparently meant greater solidarity against women and foreigners. The space of participatory politics was a gated community.

† Assemblies and court proceedings in ancient Athens took place in the *agora*, a marketplace lined by temples that also hosted the slave market. Here in embryo we see all the pillars of our society—economy, church, state, and people—and the inequality and exclusion that are intrinsic to them. We can understand the agora as a unified zone of competition, in which four interchangeable currencies delineate graduated power imbalances. The Athenian assembly was known as the Ekklēsia, the same word that later denoted the Christian Church as a whole—two historically interlinked ways of defining the social body that counts as "the people."

We can map the boundaries of this gated community in the Athenian opposition between public and private—between *polis* and *oikos*.* The *polis*, the Greek city-state, was a space of public discourse in which all citizens were considered equals, at least in theory. By contrast, the *oikos*, the household, was a hierarchical space in which male property owners ruled supreme—a zone outside the purview of the political, yet serving as its foundation. In this dichotomy, the *oikos* represents everything that provides the resources that sustain politics, yet is taken for granted as preceding and therefore outside it.

These categories remain with us today. The words *politics* ("the affairs of the city") and *police* ("the administration of the city") come from *polis,* while *economy* ("the management of the household") and *ecology* ("the study of the household") derive from *oikos.*

Democracy is still premised on this division. As long as there is a political distinction between public and private, everything from the household (the gendered space of intimacy that sustains the prevailing order with invisible and unpaid labor[†]) to entire continents and peoples (like Africa during the colonial period—or even blackness itself[‡]) may be relegated outside the sphere of politics. Likewise, the institution of property and the market economy it produces, which have served as the substructure of democracy since its origins, are placed beyond question at the same time as they are enforced and defended by the political apparatus.

* For more on this subject, consult Angela Mitropoulos's *Contract and Contagion: From Biopolitics to Oikonomia.*

† In this context, arguing that "the personal is political" constitutes a feminist rejection of the dichotomy between *oikos* and *polis*. But if this argument is understood to mean that the personal, too, should be subject to democratic decision-making, it only extends the logic of government into additional aspects of life. The real alternative is to affirm *multiple sites of power*, arguing that legitimacy should not be confined to any one space, so decisions made in the household are not subordinated to those made in the sites of formal politics.

‡ Cf. Frank B. Wilderson, III, "The Prison Slave as Hegemony's (Silent) Scandal."

Fortunately, ancient Athens is not the only reference point for egalitarian decision-making. A cursory survey of other societies reveals plenty of other examples, many of which are not predicated on exclusivity or coercion. But should we understand these as *democracies,* too?

In his *Fragments of an Anarchist Anthropology,* David Graeber takes his colleagues to task for identifying Athens as the origin of democracy; he surmises that the Six Nations, Amazigh, Sulawezi, or Tallensi models do not receive as much attention simply because none of them center around voting. On one hand, Graeber is right to direct our attention to societies that focus on building consensus rather than practicing coercion: many of these embody the best values associated with democracy much more than ancient Athens did. On the other hand, it doesn't make sense for us to label these examples truly democratic while challenging the democratic credentials of the Greeks who invented the term. This is still ethnocentricism: affirming the value of non-Western examples by granting them honorary status in our own admittedly inferior Western paradigm.* Instead, let's concede that democracy, as a specific historical practice dating from Sparta and Athens and emulated worldwide, has not lived up to the standard set by many of these other societies, and it does not make sense to describe them as democratic. It would be more responsible, and more precise, to describe and honor them in their own terms.

* Some of this confusion comes of Graeber simply equating democracy with "processes of egalitarian decision-making," as he does in his essay "There Never Was a West." Graeber acknowledges in passing that the tradition dating back to Greece is distinguished from the other examples of egalitarian decision-making he cites by the centrality of voting, but he doesn't follow up on this difference. Consequently, he arrives at a paradox: "For the last two hundred years, democrats have been trying to graft ideals of popular self-governance onto the coercive apparatus of the state. In the end, the project is simply unworkable. States cannot, by their nature, ever truly be democratized." But ancient Athens was also a state, and no less fundamentally coercive than the democracies of today. The problem is not that, as Graeber argues, "The democratic state was always a contradiction," but that Graeber has not resolved the contradictions in his own political taxonomy.

That leaves us with Athens as the original democracy, after all. What if Athens became so influential not because of how free it was, but because of how it harnessed participatory politics to the power of the state? At the time, most societies throughout human history had been stateless; some were hierarchical, others were horizontal, but no stateless society had the centralized power of *kratos*. The states that existed, by contrast, were hardly egalitarian. The Athenians innovated a hybrid format in which horizontality coincided with exclusion and coercion. If you take it for granted that the state is desirable or at least inevitable, this sounds appealing. But if the state is the root of the problem, then the slavery and patriarchy of ancient Athens were not early irregularities in the democratic model, but indications of the power imbalances coded into its DNA from the beginning.

Democracy is a Trojan horse bearing the power imbalances inherent in the state into the *polis* in the guise of self-determination.

Representative Democracy— A Market for Power

The US government has more in common with the republic of ancient Rome than with ancient Athens. Rather than governing directly, Roman citizens elected representatives to head up a complex bureaucracy. As Roman territory expanded and wealth flooded in, small farmers lost their footing and massive numbers of the dispossessed flooded the capital; unrest forced the Republic to extend voting rights to wider and wider segments of the population, yet political inclusion did little to counteract the economic stratification of Roman society. All this sounds eerily familiar.

The Roman Republic came to an end when Julius Caesar seized power; from then on, Rome was ruled by emperors. Yet very little changed for the average Roman. The bureaucracy, the military, the economy, and the courts continued to function the same as before.

Fast-forward eighteen centuries to the American Revolution. Outraged about "taxation without representation," North American subjects of the British Empire rebelled and established a representative democracy of their own,* soon complete with a Roman-style Senate. Yet once again, the function of the state remained unchanged. Those who had fought to throw off the king discovered that taxation *with* representation was little different. The result was a series of uprisings including Shay's Rebellion (1786-87), the Whisky Rebellion (1794), and Fries's Rebellion (1799-1800), all of which were brutally suppressed. The new democratic government succeeded in pacifying the

---

* This is a fundamental paradox of democratic governments: established by a crime, they sanctify law—legitimizing a new ruling order as the fulfillment and continuation of a revolt.

"Those persons who believe in the sharpest distinction between democracy and monarchy can scarcely appreciate how a political institution may go through so many transformations and yet remain the same. Yet a swift glance must show us that in all the evolution of the English monarchy, with all its broadenings and its revolutions, and even with its jump across the sea into a colony which became an independent nation and then a powerful State, the same State functions and attitudes have been preserved essentially unchanged."

– Randolph Bourne, *The State*

population where the British Empire had failed, thanks to the loyalty of many ordinary citizens who had revolted against the king. This time, they sided with the authorities: for didn't this new government *represent* them?[†]

This tragedy has been repeated time and time again. In the French revolution of 1848, the provisional government's prefect of police entered the office vacated by the king's prefect of police and took up the same papers his predecessor had just set down. In the 20th century transitions from dictatorship

[†] "Obedience to the law is true liberty," reads one memorial to the soldiers who suppressed Shay's Rebellion.

"A Constituent Assembly is the means used by the privileged classes, when a dictatorship is not possible, either to prevent a revolution, or, when a revolution has already broken out, to stop its progress with the excuse of legalizing it, and to take back as much as possible of the gains that the people had made during the insurrectional period."

– Errico Malatesta, "Against the Constituent Assembly as against the Dictatorship"

to democracy in Greece, Spain, and Chile, and more recently in Tunisia and Egypt, social movements that overthrew dictators had to go on fighting against the very same police under the democratic regime. This is *kratos,* what Bill Moyers calls the Deep State, carrying over from one regime to the next.

Laws, courts, prisons, intelligence agencies, tax collectors, armies, police: most of the instruments of coercive power that we consider oppressive in a monarchy or a dictatorship operate no differently in a democracy. That's why the same government can seamlessly transition back and forth between imposing the decisions of a minority and enforcing majority rule. Yet when we are permitted to cast ballots about who supervises these institutions, we're more likely to regard them as *ours,* even when they're used against us. This is the great achievement of two and a half centuries of democratic revolutions: instead of abolishing the means by which kings governed, they rendered those means *popular.*

The transfer of power from rulers to assemblies has served to prematurely halt revolutionary movements ever since the American Revolution. Rather than making the changes they sought via direct action, the rebels entrusted that task to their new representatives at the helm of the state—only to see their dreams betrayed.

The state is powerful indeed, but one thing it cannot do is deliver freedom to its subjects. It cannot do this because it derives its very being from their subjection. It can subject others, it can commandeer and concentrate resources, it can impose dues and duties, it can dole out rights and concessions—the consolation prizes of the governed—but it cannot offer self-determination. *Kratos* can dominate, but it cannot liberate.

Instead, representative democracy promises us the opportunity to rule each other on a rotating basis: a distributed and temporary kingship as diffuse, dynamic, and yet hierarchical as the stock market. In practice, since this rule is delegated, there are still rulers who wield tremendous power relative to everyone else; usually, like the Bushes and Clintons, they hail from a de facto ruling class. Unsurprisingly, this ruling class tends to occupy the upper echelons of all the other hierarchies of our society, both formal and informal. Even if a politician grew up among the plebs, the longer he exercises authority, the more his interests will diverge from those of the governed. Yet the real problem is not the intentions of specific politicians; it is the apparatus of the state.

Competing for the right to direct the coercive power of the state, the contestants never question the value of the state itself, even if in practice they only find themselves on the receiving end of its force. Representative democracy offers a pressure valve: when people are dissatisfied, they set their sights on the next elections, taking the state itself for granted. Indeed, if you want to put a stop to corporate profiteering or environmental devastation, isn't the state the only instrument powerful enough to accomplish that? Never mind that it was state that established the conditions in which those are possible in the first place.

So much for democracy and political inequality. What about the economic inequality that has attended democracy

since the beginning? You would think that a system based on majority rule would tend to reduce the disparities between rich and poor, seeing as the poor constitute the majority. Yet, just as in ancient Rome, the current ascendancy of democracy is matched by enormous gulfs between the haves and the have-nots. How can this be?

Just as capitalism succeeded feudalism in Europe, representative democracy proved more sustainable than monarchy because it offered mobility within the hierarchies of the state. The dollar and the ballot are both mechanisms for distributing power hierarchically in a way that takes pressure off the hierarchies themselves. In contrast to the political and economic stasis of the feudal era, capitalism and democracy ceaselessly reapportion power. Thanks to this dynamic flexibility, the potential rebel has better odds of improving his status within the prevailing order than of toppling it. Consequently, opposition tends to reenergize the political system from within rather than threatening it.

"Free election of masters does not abolish the masters or the slaves. Free choice among a wide variety of goods and services does not signify freedom if these goods and services sustain social controls over a life of toil and fear—that is, if they sustain alienation. And the spontaneous reproduction of superimposed needs by the individual does not establish autonomy; it only testifies to the efficacy of the controls."

– Herbert Marcuse, *One-Dimensional Man*

Representative democracy is to politics what capitalism is to economics. The desires of the consumer and the voter are represented by currencies that promise individual empowerment yet relentlessly concentrate power at the top of the social pyramid. As long as power is concentrated there, it is easy enough to block, buy off, or destroy anyone who threatens the pyramid itself.

This explains why, when the wealthy and powerful have seen their interests challenged through the institutions of democracy, they have been able to suspend the law to deal with the problem—witness the gruesome fates of the brothers Gracchi in ancient Rome and Salvador Allende in modern Chile,

DEMOCRACY MEANS **100%** OF THE POPULATION COOPERATING TO SECURE **51%** OF THE ELECTORATE THE RIGHT TO CHOOSE WHO GETS TO TELL EVERYONE WHAT TO DO. IN PRACTICE, OF COURSE, THAT MEANS—*ME.*

politicians who came to power via democratic elections only to be overthrown for threatening to redistribute wealth. Within the framework of the state, property has always trumped democracy.*

* The "libertarian" capitalist claims that the activities of even the most democratic government interfere with the pure functioning of the free market, while the partisan of pure democracy can be sure that as long as there are economic inequalities, the wealthy will always wield disproportionate influence over even the most carefully constructed democratic process. In fact, both the libertarian capitalist and the pure democrat are chasing will-o'-the-wisps, for government and economy are inseparable. The market relies upon the state to enforce property rights, while at bottom, democracy is a means of transferring, amalgamating, and investing political power: it is a market for agency itself.

"In representative democracy as in capitalist competition, everyone supposedly gets a chance but only a few come out on top. If you didn't win, you must not have tried hard enough! This is the same rationalization used to justify the injustices of sexism and racism: look, you lazy bums, you could have been Bill Cosby or Hillary Clinton if you'd just worked harder. But there's not enough space at the top for all of us, no matter how hard we work.

When reality is generated via the media and media access is determined by wealth, elections are simply advertising campaigns. Market competition dictates which lobbyists gain the resources to determine the grounds upon which voters make their decisions. Under these circumstances, a political party is essentially a business offering investment opportunities in legislation. It's foolish to expect political representatives to oppose the interests of their clientele when they depend directly upon them for power."

– CrimethInc. Workers' Collective, *Work*

Direct Democracy I: Let the Smartphones Decide?

"True democracy exists only through the direct participation of the people, and not through the activity of their representatives. Parliaments have been a legal barrier between the people and the exercise of authority, excluding the masses from meaningful politics and monopolizing sovereignty in their place. People are left with only a façade of democracy, manifested in long queues to cast their election ballots."

– Mu'ammer al Gaddafi, *The Green Book*

That brings us to the present. Africa and Asia are witnessing new movements in favor of democracy; meanwhile, many people in Europe and the Americas who are disillusioned by the failures of representative democracy have pinned their hopes on direct democracy, shifting from the model of the Roman Republic back to its Athenian predecessor. If the problem is that government is unresponsive to our needs, isn't the solution to make it more participatory, so we wield power directly rather than delegating it to politicians?

Electronic democracy.

But what does that mean, exactly? Does it mean regular referendums, like the one that produced the Brexit?* Does it mean voting on laws rather than legislators? Does it mean toppling the prevailing government and instituting a government of federated assemblies in its place? Or something else?

On one hand, if direct democracy is just a more participatory and time-consuming way to pilot the state, it might offer us more say in the details of government, but it will preserve the centralization of power that is inherent in it. There is a problem of scale here: can we imagine 219 million eligible voters directly conducting the activities of the US government? The conventional answer is that local assemblies would send representatives to regional assemblies, which in turn would send representatives to a national assembly—but there, already, we are speaking about representative democracy again. At best, in place of periodically electing representatives, we can picture a ceaseless series of referendums decreed from on high.

---

* In June 2016, Britain voted in a referendum to exit the European Union. Hailed by nationalists as a triumph for direct democracy, this inspired the far-right parties of the Netherlands and Germany to add regular referendums to their party platforms.

One of the most robust versions of that vision is digital democracy, or e-democracy, promoted by the various Pirate Parties. In theory, we can imagine a population linked through digital technology, making all the decisions regarding their society via majority vote in real time. In such an order, majoritarian government would gain a practically irresistible legitimacy; yet the greatest power would likely be concentrated in the hands of the technocrats who administered the system. Coding the algorithms that determined which information and which questions came to the fore, they would shape the conceptual frameworks of the participants a thousand times more invasively than election-year advertising does today.

But even if such a system could be made to work perfectly—do we want to retain centralized majoritarian rule in the first place? The mere fact of being participatory does not render a political process any less coercive. As long as the majority has the capacity to force its decisions on the minority, we are talking about a system identical in spirit with the one that governs the US today—a system that would also require prisons, police, and tax collectors, or else other ways to perform the same functions. If it is difficult to rally people against racist policing today, think how much more difficult it would be to argue that such policing is illegitimate if the citizens of a predominantly white community were directing police operations through their smart phones, democratically.

Real freedom is not a question of how participatory the process of answering questions is, but of the extent to which we can frame the questions ourselves—and whether we can stop others from imposing their answers on us. The institutions that operate under a dictatorship or an elected government are no less oppressive when they are employed directly by a majority without the mediation of representatives. In the final analysis, even the most directly democratic state is better at concentrating power than maximizing freedom.

"The digital project of reducing the world to representation converges with the program of electoral democracy, in which only representatives acting through the prescribed channels may exercise power. Both set themselves against all that is incomputable and irreducible, fitting humanity to a Procrustean bed. Fused as electronic democracy, they would present the opportunity to vote on a vast array of minutia, while rendering the infrastructure itself unquestionable—*the more participatory a system is, the more 'legitimate.'*"

-CrimethInc., "Deserting the Digital Utopia"

"Democracy is not, to begin with, a form of State. It is, in the first place, the reality of the power of the people that can never coincide with the form of a State. There will always be tension between democracy as the exercise of a shared power of thinking and acting, and the State, whose very principle is to appropriate this power ... The power of citizens is, above all, the power for them to act for themselves, to constitute themselves into an autonomous force. Citizenship is not a prerogative linked to the fact of being registered as an inhabitant and voter in a country; it is, above all, an exercise that cannot be delegated."

– Jacques Rancière,
interviewed in *Público,* January 15, 2012

Direct Democracy II: Government without the State?

Not everyone believes that democracy is a means of state governance. Some proponents of democracy have attempted to transform the discourse, arguing that true democracy is irreconcilable with state structures. For opponents of the state, this appears to be a strategic move, in that it appropriates all the legitimacy that has been invested in democracy across three centuries of popular movements and self-congratulatory state propaganda. Yet there are three fundamental problems with this approach.

First, it's ahistorical. Democracy originated as a form of state government; practically all the familiar historical examples of democracy were carried out via the state or at least by people who aspired to govern. The positive associations we have with democracy as a set of abstract aspirations came later.

Second, it fosters confusion. Those who promote democracy as an alternative to the state rarely draw a meaningful distinction between the two. If you dispense with representation, coercive enforcement, and the rule of law, yet keep all the other hallmarks that make democracy a means of governing—citizenship, voting, and the centralization of legitimacy in a single decision-making structure—you end up retaining the procedures of government without the mechanisms that make them *effective*. This combines the worst of both worlds. It ensures that those who approach anti-state democracy expecting it to perform the same function as the state will inevitably be disappointed, while creating a situation in which anti-state democracy tends to reproduce the dynamics associated with state democracy on a smaller scale.

Finally, it's a losing battle. If what you mean to denote by the word democracy can only occur outside the framework of the state, it creates considerable ambiguity to use a term that has been associated with state politics for 2500 years.* Most people will assume that what you mean by democracy is reconcilable with the state after all. This sets the stage for statist parties and strategies to regain legitimacy in the public eye, even after having been completely discredited. During the anti-government protests of 2011 in Spain and Greece, the political parties Podemos and Syriza gained traction in the occupied squares of Barcelona and Athens thanks to their rhetoric about direct democracy, only to make their way into the halls of government where they are now behaving like any other political parties. They're still doing democracy, just more *efficiently* and *effectively*. Without a language that differentiates what they are doing in parliament from what people were doing in the squares, this process will recur again and again.

When we identify what we are doing when we oppose the state as the practice of *democracy*, we set the stage for our efforts to be reabsorbed back into larger representational structures. Democracy is not just a way of managing the apparatus of government, but also of regenerating and legitimizing it. Candidates, parties, regimes, and even the form of government can be swapped out from time to time when it becomes clear that they cannot solve the problems of their constituents. In this way, government itself—the source of at least some of those problems—is able to persist. Direct democracy is just the latest way to rebrand it.

* The objection that the democracies that govern the world today aren't real democracies is a variant of the classic "No true Scotsman" fallacy. If, upon investigation, it turns out that not a single existing democracy lives up to what you mean by the word, you might need a different expression for what you are trying to describe. This is like communists who, confronted with all the repressive communist regimes of the 20th century, protest that not a single one of them was properly communist. When an idea is so difficult to implement that hundreds of millions of people equipped with a considerable portion of the resources of humanity and doing their best across a period of centuries can't produce a single working model, it's time to go back to the drawing board. Give anarchists a tenth of the opportunities Marxists and democrats have had, and then we may speak about whether anarchy works!

"We must all be both rulers and ruled simultaneously, or a system of rulers and subjects is the only alternative ... Freedom, in other words, can only be maintained through a sharing of political power, and this sharing happens through political institutions."

– Cindy Milstein, "Democracy Is Direct"

Even without the familiar trappings of the state, any form of government requires some way of determining who can participate in decision-making and on what terms—once again, who counts as the *demos*. Such stipulations may be vague at first, but they will get more concrete the older an institution grows and the higher the stakes get. And if there is no way of enforcing decisions—no *kratos*—the decision-making processes of government will have no more weight than decisions people make autonomously.[†] This is the paradox of a project that seeks *government* without the state.

These contradictions are stark enough in Murray Bookchin's formulation of libertarian municipalism as an alternative to state governance.[‡] In libertarian municipalism, Bookchin explained, an exclusive and avowedly vanguardist organization governed by laws and a Constitution would make decisions by majority

[†] Without formal institutions, democratic organizations often enforce decisions by delegitimizing actions initiated outside their structures and encouraging the use of force against them. Hence the classic scene in which protest marshals attack demonstrators for doing something that wasn't agreed upon in advance via a centralized democratic process.

[‡] Cf. Bookchin's "Thoughts on Libertarian Municipalism" in *Left Green Perspectives* #41, January 2000.

vote. They would run candidates in city council elections, with the long-term goal of establishing a confederation that could replace the state. Once such a confederation got underway, membership was to be binding even if participating municipalities wanted to withdraw. Those who try to retain government without the state are likely to end up with something like the state by another name.

The important distinction is not between democracy and the state, then, but between government and self-determination. Government is the exercise of authority over a given space or polity: whether the process is dictatorial or participatory, the end result is the imposition of control. By contrast, self-determination means disposing of one's potential on one's own terms: when people engage in it together, they are not ruling each other, but fostering autonomy on a mutually reinforcing basis. Freely made agreements require no enforcement; systems that concentrate legitimacy in a single institution or decision-making process always do.

It is strange to use the word *democracy* for the idea that the state is inherently undesirable. The proper word for that idea is *anarchism*. Anarchism opposes all exclusion and domination in favor of the radical decentralization of power structures, decision-making processes, and notions of legitimacy. It is not a matter of governing in a completely participatory manner, but of making it impossible to impose any form of rule.

From the plaza to the parliament: democracy as crowd-sourced state power.

Consensus and the Fantasy of Unanimous Rule

"In the strict sense of the term, there has never been a true democracy, and there never will be ... One can hardly imagine that all the people would sit permanently in an assembly to deal with public affairs."

— Jean-Jacques Rousseau, *Of the Social Contract*

If the common denominators of democratic government are citizenship and policing—*demos* and *kratos*—the most radical democracy would expand those categories to include the whole world: universal citizenship, community policing. In the ideal democratic society, every person would be a citizen,* and every citizen would be a policeman.†

At the furthest extreme of this logic, majority rule would mean rule by consensus: not the rule of the majority, but unanimous rule. The closer we get to unanimity, the more legitimate government is perceived to be—so wouldn't rule by consensus

---

* In theory, categories that are defined by exclusion, like citizenship, break down when we expand them to include the whole world. But if we wish to break them down, why not reject them outright, rather than promising to do so while further legitimizing them? When we use the word citizenship to describe something desirable, that can't help but reinforce the legitimacy of that institution as it exists today.

† In fact, the English word "police" is derived from *polis* by way of the ancient Greek word for citizen.

This Act of
Vandalism was
NOT
authorized by
The GA

Peaceful
Protest

A disagreement
about the role
of the general
assembly during
Occupy Oakland.

be the most legitimate government of all? Then, finally, there
would be no need for police.

Obviously, this is impossible. But it's worth reflecting on
what sort of utopia this vision implies. Imagine the kind of totalitarianism it would take to produce enough cohesion to *govern* a
society via consensus process—to get *everyone* to agree. Talk
about reducing things to the lowest common denominator! If
the alternative to coercion is to abolish disagreement, surely
there must be a third path.

This problem came to the fore during the Occupy movement
in 2011. Some participants understood the general assemblies
as the *governing bodies* of the movement; from their perspective,
it was undemocratic for people to act without unanimous
authorization. Others approached the assemblies as *spaces
of encounter* without prescriptive authority: spaces in which
people could exchange influence and ideas, forming fluid
constellations around shared goals to take action. The former
felt betrayed when their fellow Occupiers engaged in tactics

> "Democracy means government by discussion, but it is only effective if you can stop people talking."

> – Clement Attlee, UK Prime Minister, 1957

that hadn't been agreed on in the general assembly; the latter countered that it didn't make sense to grant veto power to an arbitrarily convened mass including literally anyone who happened by on the street.

Perhaps the answer is that the structures of decision-making must be decentralized as well as consensus-based, so that universal agreement is unnecessary. This is a step in the right direction, but it introduces new questions. How should people be divided into polities? What dictates the jurisdiction of an assembly or the scope of the decisions it can make? Who determines which assemblies a person may participate in, or who is most affected by a given decision? How are conflicts between assemblies resolved? The answers to these questions will either institutionalize a set of rules governing legitimacy, or prioritize voluntary forms of association. In the former case, the rules will likely ossify over time into something like a state, as people refer to protocol to resolve disputes. In the latter case, the structures of decision-making will continuously shift, fracture, clash, and re-emerge in organic processes that can hardly be described as *government*. When the participants in a decision-making process are free to withdraw from it or engage in activity that contradicts the decisions, then what is taking place is not government—it is simply conversation.*

From one perspective, this is a question of emphasis. Is our goal to produce the ideal institutions, rendering them

* See Kant's argument in *Der Streit der Fakultäten* that a republic is "violence with freedom and law," whereas anarchy is "freedom and law without violence"—the law becomes a mere recommendation that cannot be enforced.

as horizontal and participatory as possible but deferring to them as the ultimate foundation of authority? Or is our goal to maximize freedom, in which case any particular institution we create is subordinate to liberty and therefore dispensable? Once more—what is more legitimate, our institutions or the needs and desires they exist to fulfill?

Even at their best, institutions are just a means to an end; they have no value in and of themselves. No one should be obliged to adhere to the protocol of any institution that suppresses her freedom or fails to meet her needs. If everyone were free to organize with others on a purely voluntary basis, that would be the best way to generate social forms that are truly in the interests of all participants: for as soon as a structure was not working for everyone involved, they would have to refine or replace it. This approach won't bring all of society into consensus, but it is the only way to guarantee that consensus is meaningful and desirable when it *does* arise.

DECENTRALIZATION? IN THEORY, IT'S A GOOD IDEA, BUT I DOUBT WE'LL REACH CONSENSUS TO IMPLEMENT IT.

The Excluded: Race, Gender, and Democracy

"We haven't benefitted from America's democracy. We've only suffered from America's hypocrisy."

– Malcolm X, "The Ballot or the Bullet"

We often hear arguments for democracy on the grounds that, as the most inclusive form of government, it is the best suited to combat the racism and sexism of our society. Yet as long as the categories of rulers/ruled and included/excluded are built into the structure of politics, coded as "majorities" and "minorities" even when the minorities outnumber the majorities, imbalances of power along race and gender lines will always be reflected as disparities in political power. This is why women, black people, and other groups still lack political leverage proportionate to their numbers, despite having ostensibly possessed voting rights for a century or more.

In *The Abolition of White Democracy,* the late Joel Olson presents a compelling critique of what he calls "white democracy"—the concentration of democratic political power in white hands by means of a cross-class alliance among those granted white privilege. But he takes for granted that democracy is the most desirable system, assuming that white supremacy is an incidental obstacle to its functioning rather than a consequence thereof. If democracy is the ideal form of egalitarian relations, why has it been implicated in structural racism* for practically its entire existence?

* See, for example, the second chapter of Kendra A. King's *African American Politics.*

Where politics is constructed as a zero-sum competition, those who hold power will be loath to share it with others. Consider the men who opposed universal suffrage and the white people who opposed the extension of voting rights to people of color: the structures of democracy did not discourage their bigotry, but gave them an incentive to institutionalize it.

Olson traces the way that the ruling class fostered white supremacy in order to divide the working class, but he neglects the ways that democratic structures lent themselves to this process. He argues that we should promote class solidarity as a response to these divisions, but (as Bakunin argued contra Marx*) the difference between the governing and the governed is itself a class difference—think of ancient Athens. Racialized exclusion has always been the flip side of citizenship.

So the political dimension of white supremacy isn't just a consequence of racial disparities in economic power—it also produces them. Ethnic and racial divisions were ingrained in our society long before the dawn of capitalism; the confiscation of Jewish property under the Inquisition financed the original colonization of the Americas, and the looting of the Americas and enslavement of Africans provided the original startup capital to jumpstart capitalism in Europe and later North America. It is possible that racial divisions could outlast the next massive economic and political shift, too—for example, as exclusive assemblies of predominantly white citizens.

There are no easy fixes for this problem. Reformers often speak about making our political system more "democratic," by which they mean more inclusive and egalitarian. Yet when their reforms are realized in a way that legitimizes and strengthens the institutions of government, this only puts more weight behind those institutions when they strike at the targeted and marginalized—witness the mass incarceration of black people since the civil rights movement. Malcolm X and other advocates of black separatism were right that a white-founded democracy would never offer freedom to black people—not

* E.g., Bakunin's critique of the Marxist theory of the state in *God and the State*.

> "By erecting a slave society, America created the economic foundation for its great experiment in democracy ... America's indispensable working class existed as property beyond the realm of politics, leaving white Americans free to trumpet their love of freedom and democratic values."
>
> – Ta-Nehisi Coates, "The Case for Reparations"

because white and black people can never coexist, but because in rendering politics a competition for centralized political power, democratic governance creates conflicts that preclude coexistence. If today's racial conflicts can ever be resolved, it will be through the establishment of new relations on the basis of decentralization, not by integrating the excluded into the political order of the included.[†]

As long as we understand what we are doing together politically as *democracy*—as government by a legitimate decision-making process—we will see that legitimacy invoked to justify programs that are functionally white supremacist, whether they are the policies of a state or the decisions of a spokescouncil. (Recall, for example, the tensions between the decision-making processes of the predominantly white general assemblies and the less white encampments within many Occupy groups.) Only when we dispense with the idea that any political process is inherently legitimate will we be able to strip away the final alibi of the racial disparities that have always characterized democratic governance.

† This far, at least, we can agree with Booker T. Washington when he said, "The Reconstruction experiment in racial democracy failed because it began at the wrong end, emphasizing political means and civil rights acts rather than economic means and self-determination."

"As long as there are police, who do you think they will harass? As long as there are prisons, who do you think will fill them? As long as there is poverty, who do you think will be poor? It is naïve to believe we could achieve equality in a society based on hierarchy. You can shuffle the cards, but it's still the same deck."

— CrimethInc., *To Change Everything*

Turning to gender, this gives us a new perspective on why Lucy Parsons, Emma Goldman, and other women argued that the demand for women's suffrage was missing the point. Why would anyone reject the option to participate in electoral politics, imperfect as it is? The short answer is that they wanted to abolish government entirely, not to make it more participatory. But looking closer, we can find some more specific reasons why people concerned with women's liberation might be suspicious of the franchise.

Let's go back to *polis* and *oikos*—the city and the household. Democratic systems rely on a formal distinction between public and private spheres; the public sphere is the site of all legitimate decision-making, while the private sphere is excluded or discounted. Throughout a wide range of societies and eras, this division has been profoundly gendered, with men dominating public spheres—ownership, paid labor, government, management, and street corners—while women and those outside the gender binary have been relegated to private spheres: the household, the kitchen, the family, child-rearing, sex work, care work, other forms of invisible and unpaid labor.

Insofar as democratic systems centralize decision-making power and authority in the public sphere, this reproduces patriarchal patterns of power. This is most obvious when women

"The history of the political activities of men proves that they have given him absolutely nothing that he could not have achieved in a more direct, less costly, and more lasting manner. As a matter of fact, every inch of ground he has gained has been through a constant fight, a ceaseless struggle for self-assertion, and not through suffrage. There is no reason whatever to assume that woman, in her climb to emancipation, has been, or will be, helped by the ballot."

– Emma Goldman, "Women Suffrage"

are formally excluded from voting and politics—but even where they are not, they often face informal obstacles in the public sphere while bearing disproportionate responsibility in the private sphere.

The inclusion of more participants in the public sphere serves to further legitimize a space where women and those who do not conform to gender norms operate at a disadvantage. If "democratization" means a shift in decision-making power from informal and private sites towards more public political spaces, the result could even erode some forms of women's power. Recall how grassroots women's shelters founded in the 1970s were professionalized through state funding to such an extent that by the 1990s, the women who had founded them could never have qualified for entry-level positions in them.

So we cannot rely on the degree of women's formal participation in the public sphere as an index of liberation. Instead, we should deconstruct the gendered distinction between public and

> "Of all the modern delusions, the ballot has certainly been the greatest ... The principle of rulership is in itself wrong: no man has any right to rule another."
>
> – Lucy Parsons, "The Ballot Humbug"

private, validating what takes place in relationships, families, households, neighborhoods, social networks, and other spaces that are not recognized as part of the political sphere. That doesn't mean formalizing those spaces or integrating them into a supposedly gender-neutral political practice, but rather legitimizing multiple ways of making decisions, recognizing multiple sites of power within society.

There are two ways to respond to male domination of the political sphere. The first is to try to make the formal public space as accessible and inclusive as possible—for example, by registering women to vote, providing child care, setting quotas of who must participate in decisions, weighting who is permitted to speak in discussions, or even, as in Rojava, establishing women-only assemblies with veto power. This strategy seeks to implement equality, but it still assumes that all power should be vested in the public sphere. The alternative is to identify sites and practices of decision-making that already empower people who do not benefit from male privilege, and grant them greater legitimacy. This approach draws on longstanding feminist traditions* that prioritize people's lives and experiences over formal structures and ideologies, recognizing the importance of diversity and valuing dimensions of life that are usually invisible.

These two approaches can coincide and complement each other, but only if we dispense with the idea that all legitimacy should be concentrated in a single institutional structure.

* See, for example, Heidi Grasswick's "Feminist Social Epistemology" in *The Stanford Encyclopedia of Philosophy* (Spring 2013 Edition)

Arguments Against Autonomy

There are several objections to the idea that decision-making structures should be voluntary rather than obligatory, decentralized rather than monolithic. We're told that without a central mechanism for deciding conflicts, society will degrade into civil war; that it is impossible to defend against centralized aggressors without a central authority; that we need the apparatus of central government to deal with oppression and injustice. Let's discuss each of these objections in turn.

In fact, centralizing power is as likely to provoke strife as to resolve it. When everyone has to gain control of the structures of the state to obtain influence over the conditions of her own life, this is bound to generate friction. In Israel/Palestine, India/Pakistan, and other places where people of various religions and ethnicities had coexisted autonomously in relative peace, the colonially imposed imperative to contend for political power within the framework of a single state has produced protracted ethnic violence. Such conflicts were common in 19th century US politics, as well—consider the early gang warfare around elections in Washington and Baltimore,† or the fight for Bleeding Kansas. If these struggles are no longer common in the US, that's not evidence that the state has *resolved* all the conflicts it generated.

Centralized government, touted as a way to conclude disputes, just consolidates power so the victors can maintain their position through force of arms. And when centralized structures collapse, as Yugoslavia did during the introduction of democracy in the 1990s, the consequences can be bloody indeed. At best, centralization only postpones strife—like a debt accumulating interest.

† For example, on June 1, 1857, members of Baltimore's Plug Uglies and several other street gangs supporting the Know-Nothing Party attacked prospective voters at Washington, DC polling stations. The fighting continued until two companies of Marines were dispatched to control them, leaving six dead and dozens injured.

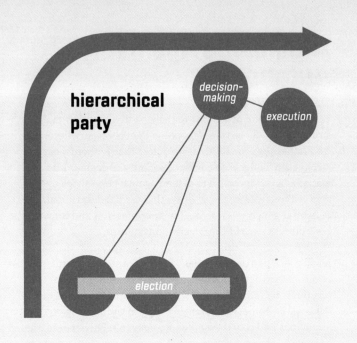

A diagram illustrating the advantages of decentralized and autonomous network-based organizing over both representative democracy and assembly-based direct democracy.

Peña-López, I. (2016) "Are assembly-based parties network parties?" In *ICTlogy*, #148, January 2016. Barcelona: ICTlogy.

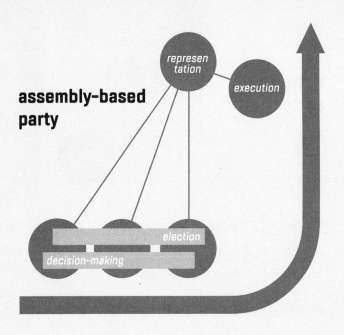

assembly-based party

representation

execution

election

decision-making

But can decentralized networks stand a chance against centralized power structures? If they can't, then the whole discussion is moot, as any attempt to experiment with decentralization will be crushed by more centralized rivals.

The answer remains to be seen, but today's centralized powers are by no means sure of their own invulnerability. Already, in 2001, the RAND Corporation was arguing* that decentralized networks, rather than centralized hierarchies, will be the power players of the 21st century. Over the past two decades, from the so-called anti-globalization movement to Occupy and the Kurdish experiment with autonomy in Rojava, the initiatives that have succeeded in opening up space for new movements and social experiments (both democratic and anarchistic) have

* In *Networks and Netwars: The Future of Terror, Crime, and Militancy*, edited by John Arquilla and David Ronfeldt.

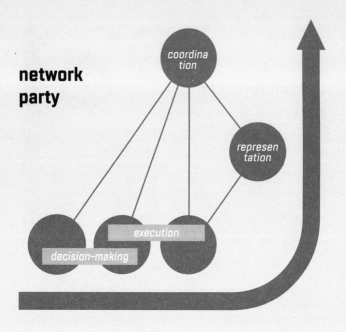

network party

coordina
tion

represen
tation

execution

decision-making

been decentralized, while more centralized efforts like Syriza have been coopted almost immediately. Scholars from many different fields of study are now theorizing the distinguishing features and advantages of network-based organizing.

Finally, there is the question of whether a society needs a centralized political apparatus to be able to put a stop to oppression and injustice. Abraham Lincoln's first inaugural address, delivered in 1861 on the eve of the Civil War, is one of the strongest expressions of this argument. It's worth quoting at length:

> Plainly the central idea of secession is the essence of anarchy. A majority held in restraint by constitutional checks and limitations, and always changing easily with deliberate changes of popular opinions and sentiments, is the only true sovereign of a free people. Whoever rejects it does of necessity fly to anarchy or to despotism. Unanimity

is impossible. The rule of a minority, as a permanent arrangement, is wholly inadmissible; so that, rejecting the majority principle, anarchy or despotism in some form is all that is left . . .

Physically speaking, we cannot separate. We cannot remove our respective sections from each other nor build an impassable wall between them. A husband and wife may be divorced and go out of the presence and beyond the reach of each other, but the different parts of our country cannot do this. They cannot but remain face to face, and intercourse, either amicable or hostile, must continue between them. Is it possible, then, to make that intercourse more advantageous or more satisfactory after separation than before? Can aliens make treaties easier than friends can make laws? Can treaties be more faithfully enforced between aliens than laws can among friends? Suppose you go to war, you cannot fight always; and when, after much loss on both sides and no gain on either, you cease fighting, the identical old questions, as to terms of intercourse, are again upon you.

This country, with its institutions, belongs to the people who inhabit it. Whenever they shall grow weary of the existing Government, they can exercise their constitutional right of amending it or their revolutionary right to dismember or overthrow it.

Follow this logic far enough in today's globalized world and you arrive at the idea of world government: majority rule on the scale of the entire planet. Lincoln is right, *contra* partisans of consensus, that unanimous rule is impossible and that those who do not wish to be ruled by majorities must choose between despotism and anarchy. His argument that aliens cannot make treaties more easily than friends make laws sounds convincing at first. But *friends* don't enforce laws on each other—laws are made to be imposed on weaker parties, whereas treaties are made between equals. *Government* is not something that takes place between friends, any more than *a free people* need a *sovereign*. If we have to choose between despotism, majority rule, and anarchy, anarchy is the closest thing to freedom—what Lincoln calls our "revolutionary right" to overthrow governments.

Yet, in associating anarchy with the secession of the Southern states, Lincoln was mounting a critique of autonomy that echoes to this day. If it weren't for the Federal government, the argument goes, slavery would never have been abolished, nor would the South have desegregated or granted civil rights to people of color. These measures against injustice had to be introduced at gunpoint by the armies of the Union and, a century later, the National Guard. In this context, advocating decentralization seems to mean accepting slavery, segregation, and the Ku Klux Klan. Without a legitimate central governing body, what mechanism could stop people from acting oppressively?

There are several errors here. The first mistake is obvious: of Lincoln's three options—despotism, majority rule, and anarchy—the secessionists represented despotism, not anarchy. Likewise, it is naïve to imagine that the apparatus of central government will be employed solely on the side of freedom. The same National Guard that oversaw integration in the South used live ammunition to put down black uprisings around the country; today, there are nearly as many black people in US prisons as there once were slaves in the US. Finally, one need not vest all legitimacy in a single governing body in order to act against oppression. One may still act—the only difference is that one does so without the pretext of enforcing law, and without having one's hands tied by it.

Opposing the centralization of power and legitimacy does not mean withdrawing into quietism. Some conflicts must take place; there is no getting around them. They follow from truly irreconcilable differences, and the imposition of a false unity only defers them. In his inaugural address, Lincoln was pleading in the name of the state to suspend the conflict between abolitionists and partisans of slavery—a conflict that was inevitable and necessary, which had already been delayed through decades of intolerable compromise. Meanwhile, abolitionists like Nat Turner and John Brown were able to act decisively without need of a central political authority—indeed, they were able to act thus only because they did not recognize one. Were it not for the pressure generated by autonomous actions like theirs, the federal government would never have intervened in the South; had more people taken the initiative the way they did, slavery would not have been possible and the Civil War would not have been necessary.

In other words, the problem was not too much anarchy, but too little. It was autonomous action that forced the issue of slavery, not democratic deliberation. What's more, had there been more partisans of anarchy, rather than majority rule, it would not have been possible for Southern whites to regain political supremacy in the South after Reconstruction.

One more anecdote bears mention. A year after his inaugural speech, Lincoln addressed a committee of free men of color to argue that they should emigrate to found another colony like Liberia in hopes that the rest of black America would follow.[*] Regarding the relation between emancipated black people and white American citizens, he argued,

> It is better for us both to be separated . . . There is an un-willingness on the part of our people, harsh as it may be, for you free colored people to remain with us.

So, in Lincoln's political cosmology, the *polis* of white citizens cannot separate, but as soon as the black slaves of the *oikos* no longer occupy their economic role, it is better that they depart. This dramatizes things clearly enough: the nation is indivisible, but the excluded are disposable. Had the slaves freed after the Civil War emigrated to Africa, they would have arrived just in time to experience the horrors of European colonization, with a death toll of ten million in Belgian Congo alone.[†] The proper solution to such catastrophes is not to integrate all the world into a single republic governed by majority rule, but to combat all institutions that divide people into majorities and minorities—rulers and ruled—however democratic they might be.

[*] See "Address on Colonization to a Deputation of Negroes" in the fifth volume of Lincoln's *Collected Works*.

[†] See, for example, Adam Hochschild's *King Leopold's Ghost: A Story of Greed, Terror, and Heroism in Colonial Africa*.

Democratic Obstacles to Liberation

"Democracy is a great way of assuring the legitimacy of the government, even when it does a bad job of delivering what the public wants. In a functioning democracy, mass protests challenge the rulers. They don't challenge the fundamental nature of the state's political system."

– Noah Feldman,
"Tunisia's Protests Are Different This Time"

Barring war or miracle, the legitimacy of every constituted government is always eroding; it can only erode. Whatever the state promises, nothing can compensate for having to cede control of our lives. Every specific grievance underscores this systemic problem, though we rarely see the forest for the trees.

This is where democracy comes in: another election, another government, another cycle of optimism and disappointment.

But this does not always pacify the population. The past decade has seen movements and uprisings all around the world—from Oaxaca to Tunis, Istanbul to Rio de Janeiro, Kiev to Hong Kong—in which the disillusioned and disaffected attempt to take matters into their own hands. Most of these have rallied around the standard of more and better democracy, though that has hardly been unanimous.

Considering how much power markets and governments wield over us, it's tempting indeed to imagine that we could

"Occasionally you rebel, but it's only ever just to start doing the same thing again from scratch."

– Albert Libertad,
"Voters: You Are the Real Criminals"

somehow turn the tables and govern *them*. Even those who do not believe that it is possible for *the people to rule the government* usually end up governing the one thing that is left to them—the ways that they rebel. Approaching protest movements as experiments in direct democracy, they set out to prefigure the structures of a more democratic world.

But what if prefiguring democracy is part of the problem? That would explain why so few of these movements have been able to mount an irreconcilable opposition to the structures that they formed to oppose. With the arguable exceptions of the Zapatistas in Chiapas and the autonomous region of Rojava, all of them have been defeated (Occupy), reintegrated into the functioning of the prevailing government (Syriza, Podemos), or, worse still, have overthrown and replaced that government without achieving any real change in society (Tunisia, Egypt, Libya, Ukraine).

When a movement seeks to legitimize itself on the basis of the same principles as state democracy, it ends up trying to beat the state at its own game. Even if it succeeds, the reward for victory is to be coopted and institutionalized—whether within the existing structures of government or by reinventing them anew. Thus movements that begin as revolts against the state end up recreating it.

This can play out in many different ways. There are movements that hamstring themselves by claiming to be more democratic, more transparent, or more representative than the authorities; movements that come to power through electoral politics, only to betray their original goals; movements that promote directly democratic tactics that turn out to be just as useful to those who seek state power; and movements that topple governments, only to replace them. Let's consider these one at a time.

If we limit our movements to what the majority of participants can agree on in advance, we may not be able to get them off the ground in the first place. When much of the population has accepted the legitimacy of the government and its laws, most people don't feel entitled to do anything that could challenge the existing power structure, no matter how badly it treats them. Consequently, a movement that makes decisions by majority vote or consensus may have difficulty agreeing to utilize any but the most symbolic tactics—with the consequence that, since it can exert no leverage to achieve its objectives, few are interested in participating.

Consider the uprising that took place in Ferguson, Missouri in August 2014 in response to the murder of Michael Brown. Can you imagine the residents of Ferguson holding a consensus meeting to decide whether to burn the QuikTrip store and fight off the police? And yet those were the actions that sparked what came to be known as the Black Lives Matter movement. People usually have to experience something new to be open to it; it is a mistake to confine an entire movement to what is already familiar to the majority of participants.

By the same token, if we insist on our movements being completely transparent, that means letting the authorities dictate which tactics we can use. In conditions of widespread infiltration and surveillance, conducting all decision-making in public without the option of anonymity invites repression on anyone who is perceived as a threat to the status quo. The more public and transparent a decision-making body is, the more conservative its actions are likely to be, even when this contradicts its express reason for being—think of all the environmental coalitions that have never taken a single step to halt the activities that cause climate change. Within democratic logic, it makes sense to demand transparency from the government, as it is supposed to represent and answer to the people. But outside that logic, rather than demanding

Hitler himself came to power in a democratic election.

that participants in social movements represent and answer to each other, we should seek to maximize the autonomy with which they may act.

If we claim legitimacy for our movements on the grounds that we represent the public, we offer the authorities an easy way to outmaneuver us, while opening the way for others to coopt our efforts. Before the introduction of universal suffrage, it was possible to maintain that a movement represented the will of the people; but nowadays an election can draw more people to the polls than even the most massive movement can mobilize into the streets. The winners of elections will always be able to claim to represent more people than can participate in movements.[*]

* At the end of May 1968, for example, the announcement of snap elections broke the wave of wildcat strikes and occupations that had swept across France; the spectacle of the majority of French citizens voting for President de Gaulle's party was enough to dispel all hope of revolution. This illustrates how elections serve as a pageantry that *represents* citizens to each other as willing participants in the prevailing order.

Likewise, movements purporting to represent the most oppressed sectors of society can be outflanked by the inclusion of token representatives of those sectors in the halls of power. And as long as we validate the idea of representation, some new politician or party can use our rhetoric to get into office. We should not claim that we represent the people—we should assert that no one has the right to represent us.

What happens when a movement comes to power through electoral politics? The victory of Luiz Inácio Lula da Silva and his Workers' Party in Brazil seemed to present a best-case scenario in which a party based in grassroots radical organizing took the helm of the state. At the time, Brazil hosted some of the world's most powerful social movements, including the 1.5-million-strong land reform campaign MST (Landless Workers' Movement); many of these were interconnected with the Workers' Party. Yet after Lula took office in 2002, social movements entered a precipitous decline that lasted until 2013. Members of the Workers' Party dropped out of local organizing to take positions in the government, while the necessities of realpolitik prevented Lula from granting concessions to the movements he had previously supported. The MST had forced the conservative government that preceded Lula to legalize many land occupations, but it made no headway whatsoever under Lula.

This pattern recurred all around Latin America as supposedly radical politicians betrayed the social movements that had put them in office. As of 2016, the most powerful social movements in Brazil were the right-wing protests that toppled the Workers' Party with a coup; grassroots movements were forced to choose between sitting on the sidelines and mobilizing behind the doomed party that had betrayed them. There are no electoral shortcuts to freedom.

What if instead of seeking state power, we focus on promoting directly democratic models such as neighborhood assemblies? Unfortunately, such practices can be appropriated to serve a wide range of agendas. In 2009, members of the Greek fascist party Golden Dawn joined locals in the Athenian neighborhood of Agios Panteleimonas in organizing an assembly that coordinated attacks on immigrants and anarchists. After the Slovenian uprising of

2012, while self-organized neighborhood assemblies continued to meet in Ljubljana, an NGO financed by the city authorities began organizing assemblies in a "neglected" neighborhood as a pilot project towards "revitalizing" the area, with the explicit intention of drawing disaffected citizens back into dialogue with the government. During the Ukrainian revolution of 2014, the fascist parties Svoboda and Right Sector came to prominence in democratic protests based on the Occupy model.

If we want to foster inclusivity and self-determination, it is not enough to propagate the rhetoric and procedures of participatory democracy.* We need to spread a framework that opposes the state and other forms of hierarchical power in and of themselves.

Even explicitly revolutionary strategies can be turned to the advantage of world powers in the name of democracy. Since 2014, in Venezuela, Macedonia, Brazil, and elsewhere, we have seen state actors and vested interests channel genuine popular dissent into ersatz social movements in order to shorten the electoral cycle. Usually, the goal is to force the ruling party to resign in order to replace it with a more "democratic" government—i.e., a government more amenable to US or EU objectives. Such movements usually focus on "corruption," implying that the system would work just fine if only the right people were in power. When we enter the streets, rather than risk being the dupes of some foreign policy initiative, we should

---

* In the face of economic crises and widespread disillusionment with representative politics, we see governments offering more direct participation in decision-making to pacify the public. Just as the dictatorships in Greece, Spain, and Chile were compelled to transition to democracy to neutralize protest movements, the state is opening up new roles for those who might otherwise lead the opposition to it. If we are directly responsible for making the political system work, we will blame ourselves when it fails—not the format itself. This explains new experiments such as the "participatory" budgets local governments are implementing from Pôrto Alegre to Poznań. In practice, the participants rarely have any leverage on town officials; at most, they can act as consultants, or vote on a measly 0.1% of city funds. The real purpose of participatory budgeting and other such programs is to redirect popular attention from the failures of government to the project of making it more democratic.

not mobilize against any particular government, but against government per se.

The Egyptian revolution dramatically illustrates the dead end of democratic revolution. After hundreds had given their lives to overthrow dictator Hosni Mubarak and institute democracy, popular elections brought another autocrat to power in the person of Mohamed Morsi. A year later, in 2013, nothing had improved, and the people who had initiated the revolution took to the streets once more to reject the results of democracy, forcing the Egyptian military to depose Morsi. Today, the military remains the de facto ruler of Egypt, and the same oppression and injustice that inspired two revolutions continues. The options represented by the military, Morsi, and the people in revolt are the same ones that Lincoln described in his inaugural speech: tyranny, majority rule, and anarchy.

Here, at the furthest limit of the struggle against poverty and oppression, we always come up against the state itself. As long as we submit to being governed, the state will shift back and forth as needed between majority rule and tyranny—two expressions of the same basic principle. The state can assume many shapes; like vegetation, it can die back, then regrow from the roots. It can take the form of a monarchy or a parliamentary democracy, a revolutionary dictatorship or a provisional council; when the authorities have fled and the military has mutinied, the state can linger as a germ carried by the partisans of order and protocol in an apparently horizontal general assembly. All of these forms, however democratic, can regenerate into a regime capable of crushing freedom and self-determination.

The one sure way to avoid cooptation, manipulation, and opportunism is to refuse to legitimize any form of rule. When people solve their problems and meet their needs directly through flexible, horizontal, decentralized structures, there are no leaders to corrupt, no formal structures to ossify, no single process to hijack. Do away with the concentrations of power and those who wish to seize power can get no purchase on society. An ungovernable people may have to defend themselves against would-be tyrants, but they will never put their own strength behind any tyrant's efforts to rule.

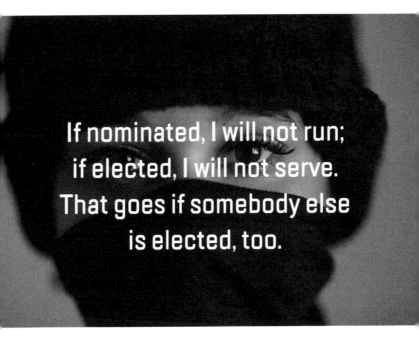

If nominated, I will not run;
if elected, I will not serve.
That goes if somebody else
is elected, too.

Towards Freedom: Points of Departure

"Anarchism represents not the most radical form of democracy, but an altogether different paradigm of collective action."

– Uri Gordon, *Anarchy Alive!*

The classic defense of democracy is that it is the worst form of government—except for all the others.* But if *government* itself is the problem, we have to go back to the drawing board.

Reimagining humanity without government is an ambitious project. Most of the models of stateless relations that sustained us through our first two hundred thousand years have been stamped out, and two centuries of anarchist theory only scratch the surface. For now, we'll suggest a few basic values that could guide us beyond democracy, and a few general proposals for how to understand what we might do instead of *governing*. Most of the work remains to be done.

* Winston Churchill, addressing the House of Commons on November 11, 1947.

Horizontality, Decentralization, Autonomy, Anarchy

Under scrutiny, democracy does not live up to the values that drew us to it in the first place: *egalitarianism, inclusivity, self-determination*. To realize these values, we must add *horizontality, decentralization*, and *autonomy* alongside them as their indispensible counterparts.

As a political aspiration, horizontality has gained a lot of currency since the late 20th century. Starting with the Zapatista uprising in Chiapas in 1994 and gaining momentum through the worldwide anti-globalization movement, a series of ostensibly horizontal grassroots social movements promoted nonhierarchical organization. The slogan *Que se vayan todos* ("They all must go!") popularized during the rebellion of 2001 in Argentina adequately expresses widespread disillusionment with politicians, parties, and leaders of all stripes. Today, the idea of leaderless structures has spread even into the business world.[†]

But decentralization is just as important as horizontality if we do not wish to be trapped in a tyranny of equals, in which everyone has to be able to agree on something for anyone to be able to do it. Rather than a single process through which all agency must pass, decentralization means multiple sites of decision-making and multiple forms of legitimacy. That way, when power is distributed unevenly in one context, this can be counterbalanced elsewhere. Decentralization means preserving difference—strategic and ideological diversity is a source of strength for movements and communities, just as biodiversity is in the natural world. We should neither reduce our politics to lowest common denominators nor segregate ourselves into homogeneous groups according to affinity alone.

Decentralization implies autonomy—the ability to act freely on one's own initiative. Autonomy can apply at any level of scale—a single person, a neighborhood, a movement, an

[†] E.g., www.holacracy.org

entire region. To be free, you need control over your immediate surroundings and the details of your daily life; the more self-sufficient you are, the more secure your autonomy is. This needn't mean meeting all your needs independently; it could also mean the kind of interdependence that gives you leverage on the people you depend on. No single institution should be able to monopolize access to resources or social relations. A society that promotes autonomy requires what an engineer would call redundancy: a wide range of options and possibilities in every aspect of life.

Yet if we wish to foster freedom, it's not enough to affirm autonomy alone.* A nation-state or political party can assert autonomy; so can nationalists and racists. The fact that a person or group is autonomous tells us little about whether the relations they cultivate with others are egalitarian or hierarchical, inclusive or exclusive. If we wish to maximize autonomy for everyone rather than simply seeking it for ourselves, we have to create a social context in which no one is able to accumulate institutional power over anyone else.

We have to create *anarchy.*

---

* "Autonomy" is derived from the ancient Greek prefix *auto-*, self, and *nomos*, law—giving oneself one's own law. This suggests an understanding of personal freedom in which one aspect of the self—say, the superego—permanently controls the others and dictates all behavior. Kant defined autonomy as self-legislation, in which the individual compels himself to comply with the universal laws of objective morality rather than acting according to his desires. By contrast, an anarchist might counter that we owe our freedom to the spontaneous interplay of myriad forces within and between us, not to the capacity to impose a single order upon ourselves. Which of those conceptions of freedom we embrace will have repercussions on everything from how we picture freedom on a planetary scale to how we understand the movements of subatomic particles—see David Graeber's excellent essay "What's the Point if We Can't Have Fun?"

"He expressed himself to us that we should never allow ourselves to be tempted by any consideration to acknowledge laws and institutions to exist as of right if our conscience and reason condemned them. He admonished us not to care whether a majority, no matter how large, opposed our principles and opinions; the largest majorities were sometimes only organized mobs."

– August Bondi, writing about John Brown

Demystifying Institutions

To say this once more: institutions exist to serve us, not the other way around. They have no inherent claim on our obedience. We should never invest them with more legitimacy than our own needs and desires. When our wishes conflict with others' wishes, we can see if an institutional process can produce a solution that satisfies everyone; but as soon as we accord an institution the right to adjudicate our conflicts or dictate our decisions, we have abdicated our freedom.

This is not a critique of a particular organizational model, or an argument for "informal" structures over "formal" ones. Rather, this insight demands that we treat all models as provisional—that we ceaselessly reappraise and reinvent them. Where Thomas Paine wanted to enthrone the law as king, where Rousseau theorized the social contract and more recent enthusiasts of capitalism *über alles* dream of a society based on contracts alone, we counter that when relations are truly in the best interests of all participants, there is no need for laws or contracts.

Likewise, this is not an argument in favor of mere individualism, nor of treating relationships as expendable, nor of organizing only with those who share our preferences. In a crowded, interdependent world, we can't afford to refuse to coexist or coordinate with others. The point is simply that we must not seek to *legislate* relations.

Instead of deferring to a blueprint or protocol, we can evaluate institutions on an ongoing basis: Do they reward cooperation—or contention? Do they distribute agency—or create bottlenecks of power? Do they offer each participant the opportunity to fulfill her potential on her own terms—or impose external imperatives? Do they facilitate the resolution of conflict on mutually agreeable terms—or punish all who run afoul of a codified system?

Creating Spaces of Encounter

In place of formal sites of centralized decision-making, we propose a variety of *spaces of encounter* where people may open themselves to each other's influence and find others who share their priorities. Encounter means mutual transformation: establishing common points of reference, common concerns. The space of encounter is not a representative body vested with the authority to make decisions for others, nor a governing body employing majority rule or consensus. It is an opportunity for people to experiment with acting in different configurations on a voluntary basis.

The spokescouncil immediately preceding the demonstrations against the 2001 Free Trade Area of the Americas summit in Quebec City was a classic space of encounter. This meeting brought together a wide range of autonomous groups that had converged from around the world to protest the FTAA. Rather than attempting to make binding decisions as a body, the participants introduced the initiatives that their groups had prepared and set out to coordinate their efforts for mutual benefit wherever possible. Much of the decision-making occurred afterwards in informal intergroup discussions. By this means, thousands of people were able to synchronize their actions without relying on central leadership or giving the police much insight into the wide array of plans that were to unfold. Had the spokescouncil employed an organizational model intended to produce unity and centralization, the participants could have spent the entire night fruitlessly arguing about which goals to embrace, which strategy to adopt, and which tactics to allow.

Most of the social movements of the past two decades have been hybrid models juxtaposing spaces of encounter with some form of democracy. In Occupy, for example, the encampments served as open-ended spaces of encounter, while the general assemblies were formally intended to function as directly democratic decision-making bodies. Most of those movements achieved their greatest effects because the encounters they facilitated opened up opportunities for autonomous action, not because they centralized group activity through direct democracy.* If we approach the *encounter* as the driving force of these movements, rather than as a raw material to be shaped through democratic process, it might help us to prioritize what we do best.

* Likewise, many of the decisions that gave Occupy Oakland a greater impact than other Occupy encampments, including the refusal to negotiate with the city government and the militant reaction to the first eviction, were the result of autonomous initiatives, not consensus process. Meanwhile, some occupiers interpreted consensus process as a sort of decentralized legal framework in which any action undertaken by any participant in the occupation required the consent of every other participant. As one participant recalls, "One of the first times the police tried to enter the camp at Occupy Oakland, they were immediately surrounded and shouted at by a group of about twenty people. Some other people weren't happy about this. The most vocal of these pacifists placed himself in front of those confronting the police, crossed his forearms in the X that symbolizes strong disagreement in the sign language of consensus process, and said 'You can't do this! I block you!' For him, consensus was a tool of horizontal control, giving everyone the right to suppress whichever of others' actions they found disagreeable."

Anarchists frustrated by the contradictions of democratic discourse have sometimes withdrawn to organize themselves according to preexisting affinity alone. Yet segregation breeds stagnation and fractiousness. It is better to organize on the basis of our conditions and needs so we come into contact with all the others who share them. Only when we understand ourselves as nodes within dynamic collectivities, rather than discrete entities possessed of static interests, can we make sense of the rapid metamorphoses that people undergo in the course of experiences like the Occupy movement—and the tremendous power of the *encounter* to transform us if we open ourselves to it.

Cultivating Collectivity, Preserving Difference

If no institution, contract, or law should be able to dictate our decisions, how do we agree on what responsibilities we have towards each other?

One proposal is to make a distinction between "closed" groups, in which the participants agree to answer to each other for their actions, and "open" groups that need not reach consensus.* But this begs the question: how do we draw a line between the two? If we are accountable to our fellows in a closed group only until we choose to leave it, and we may leave at any time, that is little different from participating in an open group. On the other hand, we are all involved, like it or not, in one closed group sharing a single inescapable space: earth. So it is not a question of distinguishing the spaces in which we must be accountable to each other from the spaces in which we may act freely. The question is how to foster both responsibility and autonomy at every order of scale.

* This is a variation on the old opposition between formal and informal; there is a hint of *polis* and *oikos* in it.

Towards this end, we can set out to create mutually fulfilling collectivities at each level of society—spaces in which people identify with each other and have cause to do right by each other. These can take many forms, from housing cooperatives and neighborhood assemblies to international networks. At the same time, we recognize that we will have to reconfigure them continuously according to how much intimacy and interdependence proves beneficial for the participants. When a configuration must change, this need not be a sign of failure: on the contrary, it shows that the participants are not competing for hegemony.

Instead of treating group decision-making as a pursuit of unanimity, we can approach it as a space for differences to arise, conflicts to play out, and transformations to occur as different social constellations converge and diverge. Disagreeing and dissociating can be just as desirable as reaching agreement, provided they occur for the right reasons; the inherent advantages of organizing in larger numbers should suffice to discourage people from fracturing gratuitously. Learning how to separate gracefully should enable us to avoid needlessly acrimonious schisms, preserving the possibility that those who part ways will later be able to come back together. Our institutions should help us to identify and understand our differences, not to suppress or submerge them.

Some witnesses returning from the autonomous regions in Rojava report that when an assembly there cannot reach consensus, it splits into two bodies, dividing its resources between them. If this is true, it offers a model of voluntary association that is a vast improvement on the Procrustean unity of democracy.

Resolving conflicts

Sometimes dividing into separate groups isn't enough to resolve conflicts. To dispense with centralized coercion, we have to come up with new ways of addressing strife. Conflicts between those who oppose the state are one of the chief assets that preserve the supremacy of the state model.* If we want to create spaces of freedom, we must not become so fractured that we can't defend those spaces, and we must not resolve conflicts in a way that creates new power imbalances.

One of the most basic functions of democracy is to offer a way of concluding disputes. Voting, courts, and police all serve to *decide* conflicts without necessarily *resolving* them; the rule of law effectively imposes a winner-take-all model for addressing differences. By centralizing force, a strong state is able to compel feuding parties to suspend hostilities even on mutually unacceptable terms. This enables a government to suppress forms of strife that interfere with its control, such as class warfare, while fostering forms of conflict that undermine horizontal and autonomous resistance, such as gang warfare. We cannot understand the religious and ethnic violence of our time without factoring in the ways that state structures provoke and exacerbate it.

When we accord institutions inherent legitimacy, this offers us an excuse not to resolve conflicts, relying instead on the intercession of the state. It gives us an alibi to conclude disputes by force and to exclude those who are structurally disadvantaged. Rather than taking the initiative to work things out directly, we end up jockeying for power.

If we don't recognize the authority of the state, we have no such excuses: we must find mutually satisfying resolutions or else suffer the consequences of ongoing strife. This is an incentive to take all parties' needs and perceptions seriously, to develop skills with which to defuse tensions and reconcile rivals. It isn't necessary to get everyone to agree, but we have to find ways to differ that do not produce hierarchies, oppression, or pointless antagonism. The first step down this

* Witness the Mexican *autodefensas*, local groups that set out to defend themselves against the cartels that are functionally identical with the government in some parts of Mexico. At first, they were able to open autonomous zones free from the violence. But then they fell out among themselves—resuming the same gang warfare that is the hallmark of capitalism and state politics, which had produced the cartel violence in the first place.

road is to remove the inducements that the state offers *not* to resolve conflict.

Unfortunately, many of the models of conflict resolution that once served human communities are now lost to us, forcibly replaced by the court systems of ancient Athens and Rome. We can look to experimental models of transformative justice for a glimpse of the alternatives that we have to develop.

Refusing to Be Ruled

Envisioning what a horizontal and decentralized society might look like, we can imagine overlapping networks of collectives and assemblies in which people organize to meet their daily needs—food, shelter, medical care, work, recreation, discussion, companionship. Being interdependent, they would have good reason to settle disputes amicably, but no one could force anyone else to remain in an arrangement that was unhealthy or unfulfilling. In response to threats, they would mobilize in larger ad hoc formations, drawing on connections with other communities around the world.

In fact, throughout the course of human history, a great many stateless societies have looked something like this. Today, models like this continue to appear at the intersections of indigenous, feminist, and anarchist traditions.[†]

That brings us back to our starting place—to modern-day Athens, Greece. In the city where democracy first came of age, thousands of people now organize themselves under anarchist banners in horizontal, decentralized networks. In place of the exclusivity of ancient Athenian citizenship, their structures are extensive and open-ended; they welcome migrants fleeing the war in Syria, for they know that their experiment in freedom must grow or perish. In place of the coercive apparatus of

† Cf. Jacqueline Lasky, "Indigenism, Anarchism, Feminism: An Emerging Framework for Exploring Post-Imperial Futures" in *Affinities: A Journal of Radical Theory, Culture, and Action*, Volume 5, Number 1 (2011)

government, they seek to maintain a decentralized distribution of power reinforced by a collective commitment to solidarity. Rather than uniting to impose majority rule, they cooperate to prevent the possibility of rule itself.

This is not an outdated way of life, but the end of a long error.

"The principle that the majority have a right to rule the minority, practically resolves all government into a mere contest between two bodies of men, as to which of them shall be masters, and which of them slaves; a contest, that—however bloody—can, in the nature of things, never be finally closed, so long as man refuses to be a slave."

– Lysander Spooner, *No Treason*

From Democracy to Freedom

Let's return to the high point of the uprisings. Thousands of us flood into the streets, finding each other in new formations that offer an unfamiliar and exhilarating sense of agency. Suddenly everything intersects: words and deeds, ideas and sensations, personal stories and world events. Certainty—finally, we feel at home—and uncertainty: finally, an open horizon. Together, we discover ourselves capable of things we never imagined.

What is beautiful about such moments transcends any political system. The conflicts are as essential as the flashes of unexpected consensus. This is not the functioning of democracy, but the experience of freedom—of collectively taking our des-

Anarchists assembling in 21st-century Athens, Greece.

tinies in our hands. No set of procedures could institutionalize this. It is a prize we must wrest from the jaws of habit and history again and again.

Next time a window of opportunity opens and we have the chance to remake our lives and our world, rather than reinventing "real democracy" once more, let us set our sights on freedom, freedom itself.

Case Studies

The following accounts were composed by participants in some of the movements that received acclaim as models of direct democracy during the global wave of rebellion between 2010 and 2014.

From 15M to Podemos

The Regeneration of Spanish Democracy

I. Emergence

Spring 2011.

"This is our revolution! No barricades, nothing romantic like that, but what do we expect? It's a piece of shit, but we already knew this is the world we live in."

I was shoulder to shoulder with a friend, pushing through the swarming crowds, the tens of thousands that had coalesced out of the democratic desolation to fill Plaça Catalunya, Barcelona's central plaza. We were on our way back from a copy shop whose employees, also taken up in the fervor, let us print another five hundred copies of the latest open letter with a huge discount, easily paid for with all the change people were leaving in the donations jar at the information table we had set up.

In less than an hour, all the pamphlets had been snatched up, we'd met more people who shared some of our ideas, had another couple engaging debates, another brief argument. Decades of social isolation had suddenly been washed away in a sudden, unexpected outpouring of social angst, anger, hope, a desire to relate. A million individual needs for the expression of collective needs: Yes, I need that, too. A million solitary voices recognizing themselves in a cry they all took up together: Yes, I am here, too. A million stories of loneliness finding themselves in a shared alienation: Yes, I feel that, too. It was hard not to get carried away. We felt it too.

But in that commune of alienation we also felt a certain cynicism. It was more than just arrogance, not merely looking down our noses at these people as they shouted every evening, "aquí comença la Revolució!"—the Revolution begins here. The truth is, we doubted the popular understanding of what a revolution would actually entail.

And our doubts were not without reason. Being out alone in the streets for years, trying to spread critical ideas, trying to open small spaces of freedom, getting handcuffed or beaten, when everyone else seems content to stare into their TV screens while the world dies around them, can certainly make you arrogant. It can make you bitter, and cynical, and superior, and completely oblivious to unexpected changes that rock the system you've spent your whole life fighting. But it can also give you perspective. It can make you ask, Why are these people in the streets now, only when their own social benefits are threatened, while they didn't lift a finger when it was other people on the chopping block? It can provoke the question, Why is the media giving so much attention to this phenomenon, even if it's often negative attention, when they've been ignoring our struggles for years?

Thousands of people fill the Plaza del Sol in Madrid during the 15M mobilization in 2011.

When the plaza occupation movement broke out on the 15th of May (15M), 2011, throughout the Spanish state, we threw ourselves into it. A few anarchists dismissed it outright, unable to find traction in that chaotic, unseemly jumble of a movement, and others uncritically gave their stamp of approval to anything that appeared to have the support of a mass. But we refused to surrender the perspectives and experiences won through years of lonely struggle when few others were insisting that the system we lived in was unacceptable.

We didn't all interpret those experiences the same way, just as we did not develop the same strategies in the midst of the plaza occupation movement. I can only give one account of this story; nonetheless it is a story we helped build collectively, struggling side by side and also disputing one another's positions. There is no consensus history of the movement, and not even of anarchist participation in it, but at the same time, no one arrived at any particular version of events alone.

One element we all shared was a critique of democracy. There was a history to our position. In 1975, Francisco Franco died. A fascist dictator who was supported by Hitler and Mussolini, and more discreetly by the British, US, and French governments, his open acceptance by the West in 1949 revealed yet again the tolerance a democratic world system can have for dictatorships that succeed in preventing revolutions. In 1976, the Basque independence group ETA blew up Franco's handpicked successor. The country was awash in wildcat strikes and protests. Armed actions were multiplying, but there was no vanguardist group with the hope of controlling or representing the whole movement. No figurehead that could be co-opted or destroyed. It was the beginning of the Transition.

Perceiving the inevitability of democratic government, the fascists turned into conservatives, constituting the Popular Party, and in exchange for legalization and a chance at power, they enticed the communists and the socialists into negotiations, giving birth to a new legalized, institutionalized labor union, CCOO, and a new political party, the Socialist Workers Party of Spain (PSOE). The PSOE ruled the country from 1982 to 1996, and in 2010 they were again in power when European

Union bureaucrats and bank financiers demanded austerity measures. They quickly complied.

But back in the mid-70s, not everyone jumped on the bandwagon. Many people rejected negotiations with fascists, or rejected any kind of government and any form of capitalism altogether. As the years turned into decades, these holdouts became ever more isolated, until they had been consigned to a political ghetto by institutional, judicial, and media marginalization. By this point, the "irreducibles" could mostly be found within an anarchist movement that was much weaker and more infirm than it had been before the Civil War that put Franco in power.

These anarchists kept fighting, largely developing an anti-social character as a tool to help them resist the psychosocial effects of extreme marginalization, and to facilitate a critique of democratic society as a majoritarian, mediatized control structure. But as revolts started breaking out in neighboring countries several years before the onset of the economic crisis, some anarchists started becoming attentive to the possibilities of a widespread social revolt, and they began changing their methods and analyses to be able to encourage and participate in such revolts, in the seemingly unlikely chance that one should break out here. In a few short years, coinciding with the beginning of the crisis, the revolts multiplied, coming closer—if not geographically, then ideologically.

Before the 15M movement, Barcelona had already witnessed a one-day general strike with majority participation, in which anti-capitalist discourses were frequent if not predominant, and which resulted in large scale occupations, rioting, looting, and clashes with police, constituting an important step in the re-appropriation of street tactics that would make other victories possible in the following years. A combative May Day protest had abandoned the typical route through the city center to snake through several rich neighborhoods, sowing destruction and a small measure of economic revenge.

The 15M movement broke out just two weeks later, and its official discourses called for total pacifism and symbolic citizen protests to achieve a better, healthier democracy through constitutional reform. Almost no mention was made, in this official discourse, of the conditions of daily life, of collective self-defense against austerity and the direct self-organization of our survival. But where did this official discourse come from, and how was it produced in such a huge, heterogeneous crowd?

15M wasn't huge from the beginning. In fact, the first assembly in Barcelona, the first night on Plaça Catalunya, there were just a hundred people present. Some of these were adherents of "Real Democracy Now," a new group based in Madrid that had produced the original call-out for the countrywide protests and occupations. Their discourse was extremely reformist and made no mention of the growing waves of real protest and social conflict that had been growing in Spain, building off a tradition of struggle that contained a great deal of collective knowledge. This history was absent from their perspective, which was perhaps the only way they could feasibly call for a movement based on pacifism and legal reform. They did mention the "Arab Spring," above all the uprising in Egypt, but only in the most condescending, manipulative way. They described it as a nonviolent movement, and they portrayed it as having already won its objectives, when, as is clear now and was clear then for anyone with a radical perspective, the struggle had only begun.

In that first assembly, they took up an old Trotskyist tactic. Distributing themselves throughout the circle, they tried to push the group to adopt a pre-ordained consensus that matched the directives that had come down from Madrid. But it was clear that these activists were not experienced in such tactics, for they were all wearing identical "Real Democracy Now" t-shirts. The minute someone from the leftwing Catalan independence movement said that the Barcelona occupation should set out on its own path rather than following Madrid, the crowd agreed. There were very few anarchists that first night, but those present also made sure that the reformist activists were not able to limit the movement from the outset.

"Who is in favor?" asks the person with the microphone, her voice booming out from concert-quality speakers. A few thousand people raise their hands.

"Who is against?" Some fifty people raise their hands. Pro forma, a few people make a rapid count. It's doubtful their numbers match up, but it doesn't matter. It is clear that the "no" votes aren't enough to be considered important. It takes a hundred to block a measure.

"Who wants more debate?" A dozen hands go up. Again, short of minimum necessary to send the proposal back for more debate.

"The proposal passes." The moderators pause a moment before moving on to the next item. The crowd, perhaps ten thousand strong, waits, sitting with a tolerant but bored patience.

"What did we just vote on?" I hear one young student ask another. Without exaggerating, I think it is one of the most common questions in that month of occupation.

Just a week into this grand experiment in direct democracy, abstention had already carried the day. In most votes, abstention reached proportions that equaled or surpassed the percentage who opt out of voting in the elections and referendums of a typical representative democracy.

It's no surprise. Empowerment was little more than a slogan in the plaza. With even a hundred people in an assembly, not everyone can participate. Once the number of participants grew from the hundreds to the thousands, commissions and subcommissions started popping up like mushrooms after a rain. Experienced moderators began directing the assemblies, putting in practice techniques for a modified consensus process that had been developed during the anti-globalization movement. Proposals were developed and consensed on in commissions, then they had to be clearly read out to be ratified by the general assembly. A hundred people, if I recall correctly, could block a decision, and a smaller number could send it back to the commission for more debate.

To truly have any meaningful influence on a decision, someone would have to spend two to four hours during the day at a commission meeting to draft the proposal, in addition to the several hours that the nighttime general assembly lasted. More difficult proposals were in commission for days or a whole week, and in any case you had to go to the commission meetings every day if you wanted to make sure that the old proposal wasn't erased by a new one. Clearly, only a small number of people with a certain level of economic independence could participate fully in these directly democratic structures. Even if everyone enjoyed economic independence, the structures themselves necessarily function as funnels, limiting and concentrating participation so that a large, heterogeneous mass can produce unified, enumerated, homogeneous decisions. In any given assembly or commission, certain styles of communication and decision-making are favored, while others are disadvantaged.

Direct democracy is just representative democracy on a smaller scale. It inevitably recreates the specialization, centralization, and exclusion we associate with existing democracies. Within four days, once the crowds exceeded 5000, the experiment in direct democracy was already rife with false and manipulated consensus, silenced minorities, increasing abstention from voting, and domination by specialists and internal politicians.

In one example, anarchists in the Self-Organization and Direct Democracy Sub-Commission wanted to organize a simple debate about nonviolence. The initiative almost failed because the Sub-Commission needed days to debate and reach consensus on exactly how they wanted to do it. In the end, two people decided to ignore the commission, and joining with another anarchist who was not participating in Self-Organization, the three of them self-organized a successful talk and debate in just a day, accomplishing what a group of fifty people had failed at over the course of a week.

It was not that easy, however, because of the many obstacles that the democracy activists put in the way of any direct action that did not have their stamp of approval. Twice, we reserved the sound system and the central space in the plaza in order to debate the nonviolence policy that had been forcibly imposed on the whole movement. Each time, our reservation mysteriously disappeared, and after the second time, the sound system was reserved for another event at the same time we had scheduled our debate. Defeated, we decided to hold the debate with just a megaphone on the edge of the plaza. It would be smaller, effectively marginalized, but we were insistent on registering our disagreement with a position that really only a small minority of activists had successfully imposed.

We went to the Activity Commission tent to again inform them of our plans. In a story worthy of Kafka, the kid at the table looked down at his form, a crappy little piece of paper written up in ballpoint pen, and told us we couldn't have our event in the spot where we wanted. "Why not?" I asked, trying not to go ballistic. Was this yet another trick by the new specialists of direct democracy to protect their false consensus around nonviolence?

The response was far more pathetic than I had expected.

"Because our forms are divided into different columns, see, one column for each space in the plaza, but that space over by the staircase, well that's not an official space."

"That's okay, we don't mind, just write it down."

"But, but, I can't. There isn't a column for it."

"Well, make a column."

"Um, I can't."

"Oh Christ, look, which one's open—look, here, 'Pink Space,' just write our event down for the 'Pink Space' and when the time comes we'll just move it."

Within two weeks, without any prior training, the Spanish Revolution had created perfect bureaucrats!

Examples of the manipulation of process abound. In the very beginning, the assembly made the very anarchist decision to not release unitary manifestos speaking for everyone. Subsequently, people spoke their own minds in the assemblies and in informal spaces throughout the day. We set up a literature table where we distributed open letters and pamphlets, publishing new texts every day. We were content to express ourselves in dialogue with the rest, rather than trying to represent the whole movement. But the grassroots politicians in the mix craved some unitary manifesto, some list of demands with which they could pressure the politicians in power. They only saw the huge crowds as numbers, means to an end.

Subsequently, they formed a Contents Commission in order to formulate the "contents" or the ideas of the movement, as though the whole plaza occupation was just an empty vessel, a mindless beast waiting for the assembly to ratify a list of common beliefs and positions. At the anarchist tent, we debated whether or not to participate in the commissions. Some of us were staunchly against, but as anarchists, we didn't seek consensus. Those who wanted to participate did not need our permission. And at least one good thing came out of their participation: many more examples of the intrinsic corruption and authoritarianism of democracy at every level.

When anarchist participation prevented the Trotskyists, Real Democracy activists, and other grassroots politicians from producing the sort of unitary demands and manifestos that the general assembly had earlier vetoed, the Commission was broken up into a dozen sub-commissions. Every single day, in multiple sub-commissions, the grassroots politicians made the same proposals that had been defeated the day before, until one meeting when none of their opponents were present. The demands were passed through the commission and

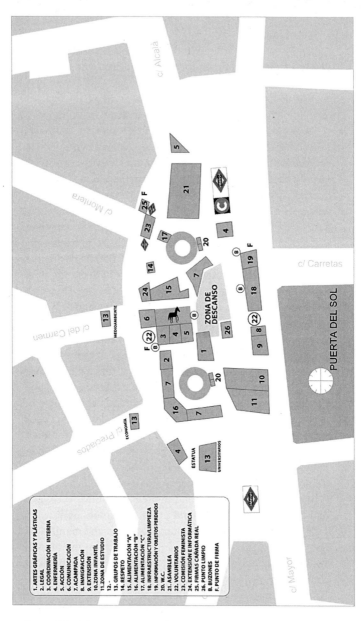

1. ARTES GRÁFICAS Y PLÁSTICAS
2. LEGAL
3. COORDINACIÓN INTERNA
4. ENFERMERÍA
5. ACCIÓN
6. COMUNICACIÓN
7. ACAMPADA
8. INMIGRACIÓN
9. EXTENSIÓN
10. ZONA INFANTIL
11. ZONA DE ESTUDIO
12. -
13. GRUPOS DE TRABAJO
14. RESPETO
15. ALIMENTACIÓN "A"
16. ALIMENTACIÓN "B"
17. ALIMENTACIÓN "C"
18. INFRAESTRUCTURA/LIMPIEZA
19. INFORMACIÓN Y OBJETOS PERDIDOS
20. W.C.
21. ASAMBLEA
22. VOLUNTARIOS
23. COMISIÓN FEMINISTA
24. EXTENSIÓN E INFORMÁTICA
25. FIRMAS CAÑADA REAL
26. PUNTO LIMPIO
B. BUZONES
F. PUNTO DE FIRMA

Map of the Plaza del Sol, May 20, 2011

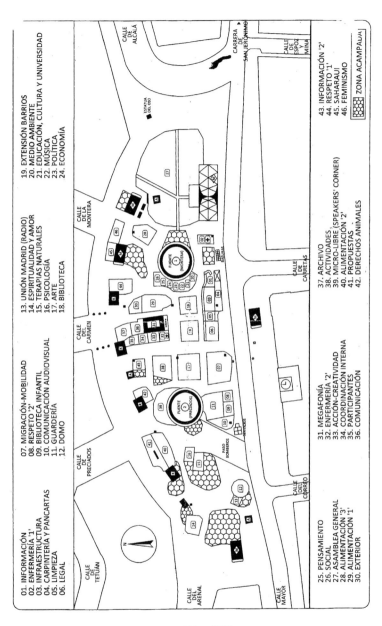

Map of the Plaza del Sol, end of May 2011

subsequently ratified by the general assembly, which ratified nearly every proposal passed before it.

On the other hand, after a week of debate, anarchists in the Self-Organization and Direct Democracy Sub-Commission reached a hard-won consensus with the proponents of direct democracy for a proposal to decentralize the assembly, meaning that heterogeneity and differences would be respected, and the assembly would be turned into a space for sharing proposals and initiatives, but not for ratifying them, because, in the new system, everyone would be free to take whatever actions they saw fit, and wouldn't need some bureaucratic permission. The proposal would have meant the utter defeat of the grassroots politicians, because the assembly would no longer be a mass they could control for their own ends. Everyone would be free to organize their own initiatives and make their own decisions. The funnel would be turned into an open field.

The anarchist proposal to decentralize the assembly was voted on twice, and each time achieved overwhelming support, but curiously was defeated on technicalities both times. The moderators hemmed and hawed, delayed and threw up obstacles. When they could no longer prevent a vote, the proposal received a greater majority than perhaps any other item in those weeks. Their tactic of trying to scare people away from the proposal, insisting that it be read several times, that everyone made sure they understand its implications, and that an extra day be granted to reflect on it backfired. In the end, this was one of the few proposals that everyone in the assembly paid attention to, discussed, and voted on with total awareness.

Only about fifty people voted against. The same fifty people voted for more debate, even though they had absolutely no intention of participating in the debate, and the proposal was effectively shelved. It had already achieved a consistent consensus in the Sub-Commission. More debate would change nothing. It would only come back before the general assembly where it would be blocked again. Thanks to direct democracy, fifty people could control twenty thousand.

This action demonstrated that we were right, we had lots of support, and the assembly was a sham—that, in itself, was a victory. But direct democracy cannot be reformed from within.

Many people took the commissions and the general assembly more seriously than they warranted. True, fruitful debates in groups of fifty or a hundred people took place in the commissions, and the assembly partially served as a platform for strangers to air their grievances and construct a sense of collectivity. But the only worthwhile position was to subvert those structures of bureaucracy and centralization, to criticize the power dynamics they created and create something more vibrant and free in the shadow of the general assembly.

There was a lot more to the plaza occupation than these frustratingly bureaucratic structures. The official center, in fact, was tiny compared to the chaotic margins. These margins were all the spaces in the plaza outside of the commission tents and the couple hours of general assembly every evening. All throughout the day, the plaza was an extensive, chaotic space of self-organization, where people met their logistical needs, sometimes going through the official channels, sometimes not. There was a library, a garden, an international translation center, a kitchen with big stoves and solar cookers, and at any time there were a couple concerts, workshops, debates, and massage parlors going on, along with innumerable smaller conversations, debates, and encounters. People drank, argued, celebrated, slept, made out, made friends.

It was chaos, in the literal sense that patterns emerged and faded, and there was no central space from which everything could be perceived, much less controlled. Consider the officially recognized program: one only had to go to the Activities Commission tent to see the whole schedule. From that one point, a police detective could register all the events taking place, what was being talked about, what was being organized. A new person wishing to take part could come and learn where to get involved, their introduction taking the form of a piece of paper, a schedule, rather than a new friend. A grassroots politician could monopolize the more important spaces and times, giving priority to certain meetings or events and marginalizing others (or they could even make undesired events disappear, as happened with our nonviolence debate). It is absolutely no coincidence that the interests of state control from without, the interests of hierarchical control from within, and the interests of impersonal or rational efficiency all converge in the structures of direct democracy.

In contrast, the unofficial margins were much livelier and more dynamic. Most new friendships and complicities, most meaningful, face-to-face conversations, and most of the satisfying communal experiences that kept people coming back occurred in the chaotic margins. A handful of people could organize a debate or a small concert without having to exhaust themselves going through commissions and subcommissions. Saving their energies for what really mattered—the actual activity—a few individuals could prepare a quality event on their own initiative, and a crowd of a hundred or even five hundred people might spontaneously gather and take part.

Even during the general assemblies, the chaotic margins could not be extinguished. Many thousands of people boycotted the votes. Some of us refused on principal to legitimate such farcical exercises of authority in the name of the people, a collective whole that was only effaced by the artificial imposition of unity. Many others didn't vote because they found the assembly boring (much like the child in the classroom who daydreams, not because she is unintelligent, but because she is, in fact, too intelligent to be engaged by an authoritarian, pacifying method of education). Still others did not participate because, once the crowds had surpassed fifty thousand, they couldn't get close enough to hear. The margins of the plaza became an unruly country of whispered conversations, criticisms, and occasional heckling.

Weren't all these other spaces also decision-making spaces? Don't we make decisions in every moment of our lives? Why is the formalized, masculine space of an assembly more legitimate than the common kitchen, where many decisions and conversations also take place? Why is it more legitimate than the hundred clusters of small conversations and debates that take place during the day, on a small scale, allowing people to express themselves more intimately and more fully?

And even if we could participate in every formal decision, would we make the same decisions we would arrive at in spaces

Speaking truth to power?

of comfort, spaces of life rather than of politics? Is it possible that our formal selves become a sort of representation, a manipulation produced during a few boring hours of meetings that is used to control us during all the other moments of our lives?

"Don't do that," says the self-appointed leader to the person who has started to spray-paint a bank, "this is a peaceful protest." The former speaks with all the legitimacy of a popular mandate. Supposedly, there is consensus on the question of nonviolence, for this protest was organized by the plaza assembly. Yet, what kind of consensus requires continual enforcement? Why did people who took part in the assembly rebel so frequently against the decisions that supposedly represented them?

Needless to say, the proponents of direct democracy and its official structures did whatever they could to suppress the chaotic zones in the plaza. The anarchist tent, for example, never had official permission, and on the first day we set up, they tried to kick us out. We made it clear that they would have to use force to get us out, and then everyone would see what their democracy consisted of. They would have done it, if we hadn't

Neighborhood assembly, May 2011.

been numerous, fierce, and honed by the years of street fighting behind us. Instead, they set up some commission tents on our spot early the next morning. But we just found another spot.

The "Convivencia" Commission ("Living Together," a classist, often racist term that is systematically used by the city's administrators) busied itself trying to eject people who were drinking in the plaza—but not the young white students, only the older, typically immigrant homeless men who were sleeping in the plaza. They also repeatedly tried kicking out the undocumented immigrants who had to work selling beers or purses in the streets, and who often had to run from the police. The Commission members tried to deny these immigrants access to the safe space we all had created in the plaza, until some of us got up in their faces, called them racists, and threatened them with physical violence.

Calling the 15M movement imperfect doesn't cut it. All the oppressive dynamics, all the habits of passivity and authoritarianism in our society followed us into the plaza. But there, in that collective space, we had the opportunity to confront them. The structures of direct democracy only masked or exacerbated those dynamics; they were feeble attempts to control the underlying chaos. Even some anarchists failed to see this. Like many others, they got distracted by the air of officiality—the titles and processes, commissions, schedules, and diagrams. All that was a farce. The imposition of an official framework was intended to redirect our attention just the same as it sought to control our participation. Next time, hopefully, we will know not to take it seriously.

In time, the 15M movement subsided, blending back into the social conflicts that gave birth to it, which continued unabated. For a while, many anarchists in Barcelona participated with thousands of other people in the neighborhood assemblies that replaced the Plaça Catalunya occupation. Home defense protests against foreclosures gained frequency. There were occupations of schools and hospitals against austerity measures. General strikes and riots. Protests against new repressive laws. Waves of arrests and counterprotests. The struggle continued.

The rise of these movements taught us a number of things. Their origins confirmed certain anarchist theories about social conflict. They were not mechanically triggered by material conditions, as they tended to precede the worst economic effects of austerity. The way I see it, material conditions do not exist, only people's interpretations of their conditions. (The whole category of the "material" seems more like a crude attempt to appear scientific, though it relies on a dichotomy that stems from the origins of Western, Christian civilization.) The true triggers of the movements included empathy for the revolts occurring in other countries, a sense of insecurity or an evaluation that the State had become weak, outrage in response to government measures seen as insulting to people's dignity and threatening to their wellbeing, and the expectation that things were getting worse.

Governments often react clumsily to emerging movements, causing them to grow and radicalize, whereas reformist or power-hungry participants are the most effective and astute in establishing statist organization within the movements and preventing them from developing revolutionary perspectives. We saw this in institutional responses to and within the movement.

Additionally, a number of hypotheses regarding pacifism were confirmed. Our society trains people to uncritically favor pacifism in social movements, and the predominant current of pacifism moves progressively away from a practice of social change towards total self-pacification; media, police, and would-be movement leaders conspire to enforce pacifism; the natural evolution of movements leads them to break with nonviolence and develop more forceful tactics. But events also gave us the opportunity to see how would-be leaders of social movements, if the crowd leaves them too far behind, will abandon their commitment to nonviolence and support or at least condone certain illegal or destructive tactics.

In contrast, the leaders' commitment to democracy runs deeper, and it was the blind support for the values of democracy that best enabled them to assert leadership over what had been a fundamentally anarchic movement.

Real Democracy Now did an excellent job of formulating a mediocre politics defined by its populism, reformism, and moralism. By using common, value-laden terms such as "democracy" (good) and "corruption" (bad), they created a discursive trap that garnered overwhelming support for all their proposals while deflecting or only pretending to include proposals that went further. Their stated minimums included revolutionary language and the highly popular sentiment that "we're going to change everything," while offering a ladder of demands that basically signaled the prices, from cheap to expensive, at which they would sell out. It started with reform of the electoral law, passed through laws for increased oversight of the bankers, and reached, at its most radical extreme, a refusal to pay back the bailout loans. Everything was structured around demands communicated to the existing government, but prettied up in populist language. Thus, the popular, anarchist slogan *Ningú ens representa*, "No one represents us," was distorted within their program to mean, "None of the politicians currently in power represent us: we want better ones who will."

However, to carry out this balancing act, they did have to adopt vaguely anti-authoritarian organizing principles inherited from the anti-globalization movement, such as a commitment to open assemblies and a rejection of spokespersons and political parties. Proposals centered on direct action or sentiments containing a rejection of government and capitalism were easily neutralized within this ideological framework. The former would be paternalistically tolerated as cute little side projects eclipsed by the major projects of reformist demands, and the latter would be applauded, linked back to the popular rhetoric already in use, and corrupted to mean an opposition to current politicians or specific bankers.

The only way to challenge this co-optation of popular rage was to focus critique on democracy itself. We quickly discovered that the idea of direct democracy was the major theoretical barrier that protected the existing representative democracy, and direct democracy activists, including anarchists, were the critical bridge between the parasitic grassroots politicians and their social host body.

The experience in the plaza taught us in practice what we had already argued in theory: that direct democracy recreates representative democracy; that it is not the features that can be reformed (campaign finance, term limits, popular referendums), but the most central ideals of democracy that are inherently authoritarian. The beautiful thing about the encampment in the plaza was that it had multiple centers for taking initiative and creating. The central assembly functioned to suppress this; had it succeeded, the occupation would have died much sooner. It did not succeed, thanks in part to anarchist intervention.

The central assembly did not give birth to a single initiative. What it did, rather, was to grant legitimacy to initiatives worked out in the commissions; but this process must not be portrayed in positive terms. This granting of legitimacy was in fact a robbing of the legitimacy of all the decisions made in the multiple spaces throughout the plaza not incorporated into an official commission. Multiple times, self-appointed representatives of this or that commission tried to suppress spontaneous initiatives that did not bear their stamp of legitimacy. At other

They call it democracy.

times, commissions, moderators, and internal politicians specifically contravened decisions made in the central assembly, when doing so would favor further centralization. This is not a question of corruption or bad form; democracy always subverts its own mechanisms in the interests of power.

Again and again in the plaza, we saw a correlation between democracy and the paranoia of control: the need for all decisions and initiatives to pass through a central point, the need to make the chaotic activity of a multitudinous occupation legible from a single vantage point—the control room, as it were. This is a statist impulse. The need to impose legibility on a social situation—and social situations are always chaotic—is shared by the democracy activist, who wishes to impose a brilliant new organizational structure; the tax collector, who needs all economic activity to be visible so it can be re-appropriated; and the policeman, who desires a panopticon in order to control and punish. I also found that numerous anarchists of various ideological stripes were unable to see the crucial theoretical difference between the oppositions *representational democracy vs. direct democracy/consensus* and *centralization vs. decentralization,* because the first and second terms of both pairs have been turned into synonyms through misuse. For this reason, I have decided to rehabilitate the term "chaos" in my personal usage, as it is a frightening term no populist in the current context would use and abuse, and it relates directly to mathematical theories that express the kind of shifting, conflictual, constantly regenerating, acephalous organization anarchists are calling for.

II. Ossification

Fall 2015.

Junts pel Sí, the pro-independence coalition that combines the major right-wing and left-wing political parties in Catalunya, has won the regional elections. Together with the CUP—a grassroots activist platform that makes decisions in assemblies, and which emerged from the social movements to seize over 10% of the vote—they have a majority in the Catalan parliament, and they have announced that they will make a unilateral declaration of independence, turning the parliament into a constituent assembly for a new constitution, breaking away from Spain. Meanwhile, the Popular Party and Socialist Party, which until four years ago ruled the country in an unshakeable two-party system, threaten legal action from Madrid. Podemos, an activist political party modeled on the Greek party Syriza, promises a referendum on independence for Catalunya, the Basque country, and Galicia, if only they are voted into power. They hint at the possibility of a new constitution, transforming Spain into a nation of nations. The newspapers and the TV are full of it every day. Everyone waits, expectantly.

In the spring, activist platforms, some of them barely a year old, won the elections in Madrid, Valencia, and Barcelona. In Donostia, the newly legalized Basque independence party, Bildu, was already in power. These constitute four of Spain's most important cities, including the two largest.

The new mayor of Barcelona, Ada Colau, had been a housing activist who once got arrested in a highly publicized act of

Madrid's Plaza del Sol, once again filled with people, during a rally called by Podemos in 2015.

civil disobedience to stop an eviction. People everywhere talk about whether she will deliver on her promises and protect all the families who can no longer pay mortgages from getting kicked out their houses. Will she create dignified employment? Will she halt the ravages of tourism that are remaking the city? Everyone waits, expectantly.

A new anarchist text from Barcelona, "A Wager on the Future," argues that these new political parties are the result of the death of the 15M movement. The would-be leaders did not succeed in directly turning the movement into a new political party, although they certainly tried. Across the country, hundreds of thousands of people gave self-organization in assemblies a chance—and on the face of it, they achieved nothing. A couple years later, in a climate of general disappointment, passivity, and demobilization, Podemos and the other new political parties such as Barcelona en Comú appeared. Preexisting activist platforms-turned-political-parties, like the CUP or Compromís in Valencia, geared up to seize a bigger slice of pie. The few remaining neighborhood assemblies or 15M assemblies, bare skeletons, became recruiting tools for one party or another.

Spanish democracy has been regenerated. People, having failed themselves, are once again ready to place their trust in politicians, as long as they are new faces making new promises. Direct democracy has revealed how fully it transforms back into representative democracy as it scales up.

At this juncture, we can see how direct democracy protected and revitalized representative democracy. Coherent with its emphasis on formal, superficial, and regulated participation in an alienated space of politics—the central assembly as the arbiter of all social decision-making—the direct democracy movement pushed for a set of demands based on institutional reform and social consensus.

What does this mean in the details of everyday life and struggle? Like all other forms of government, direct democracy preserves and even celebrates politics as an alienated sphere of life; in fact, politics—the management of the polis—is in its origins directly democratic. In one of the original alienations, people are made spectators to the decisions that determine how they live.

Assemblies are a great way to make certain decisions in specific situations, but direct democracy gives precedence to the general assembly over the affinity group, over the kitchen, over the study circle, over the workshop, and over a thousand other spaces in which we organize ourselves. This is an exact parallel to how all governments bestow an exclusive legitimacy on whatever form of decision-making they control within institutional channels. A government run by charismatic statesmen will give precedence to a congress or parliament, a government run by technocrats will give precedence to central banks and state commissions . . . and a government run by grassroots activists on their way to professionalization will give precedence to the assembly.

In the Russian revolution of 1917, one of the genre-setting revolutions of the modern era, the Bolsheviks made use of the soviets—which functioned as democratic assemblies and which contemporary anarchists like Voline pointed out were ripe for co-optation—until they had consolidated their bureaucratic state enough to no longer need the earlier structure. The compatibility between what was a direct or at least a federated democracy and the "democratic centralism" that latched onto the former and took it over should not escape us. It's not ancient history, but a pattern that keeps repeating.

Direct democracy is differentiated from other forms of government through an emphasis on the principle of "self-government." Anti-authoritarians who advocate direct democracy might avoid this term, but in fact it is quite accurate. Direct democracy involves people in their own government, which is to say their alienation from social decision-making. We can see this in how people in Plaça Catalunya ended up abstaining or going through the motions in the nightly assemblies. By being given an opportunity for self-government, they were being reeducated, in a very direct, accurate, and hands-on way, as to exactly what government means. It is no coincidence that in the aftermath, a huge proportion of these masses were once again ready to support a political party and reproduce all the same problems of disempowerment and alienation that had brought them out into the plazas in the first place.

When anarchists direct our anger and criticism at the proponents of direct democracy, it is not because we are so dogmatic, so infatuated with navel-gazing or with purifying our tiny spaces of dissidence that we would rather attack an ally than go up against the real bad guys in the banks, board rooms, and parliaments. On the contrary, it is because the movement for direct democracy constitutes the most effective appendage of the State within our struggles for liberation. After all, we are not just victims. We live in an oppressive society because every day we help to reproduce that oppression. It is for this reason we criticize. Just as a limited "self-management" in the workplace turns you into your own boss, self-government turns you into your own ruler, and there is nothing sadder than being the active agent in your own alienation. In sum, self-government means being your own worst enemy.

That is why it was logical for a movement based in direct democracy to advocate demands based on institutional reform and social consensus: the movement's sights were already fixed on seizing centralized power—the power that stems from our alienation and powerlessness—rather than destroying it. Instead of proposing an end to the ruling institutions, direct democracy activists proposed ways to fix them. Rather than seeking the abolition of hierarchical society, rather than choosing sides in the antagonisms of class, colonialism, and patriarchy, they sought social unity. After all, society is the machine that politicians wish to drive, so it makes no sense for would-be politicians to try to dismantle it.

This reformist bent diverted the movement from a collision course with authority. The values of direct democracy suppressed a more radical conflict that had been brewing, as seen in the riots of May Day 2011 and the general strikes of September 29, 2010, January 27, 2011, and especially March 29, 2012. It is that conflict which serves as a laboratory, as a cauldron for revolution. By limiting the conflict, the movement for democracy put a handicap on our collective learning process and robbed us of the experiences that might have offered a glimpse of a revolutionary horizon, one without rulers, without exploitation, without domination.

The reformist promises of the would-be leaders achieved something else. By redirecting attention to the question of the bail-outs, public funds, government corruption, and so on, they distracted people from the vital possibility of responding to austerity on the terrain of daily life, with the collective self-organization of our needs. And because no reform was achieved through the assemblies, most people experienced them as failures. Interesting and inspiring, but failures nonetheless. Surely the pragmatists were right in saying that self-organization on the scale of society is an idealistic utopia.

This bait-and-switch blinded many people to the advances that the assemblies did achieve. They constituted an important first step—meeting one another, starting the great social conversation—towards the self-organization of life. And they served as a tool to increase our power, our ability to take over public space and transform it into communal space. In the struggle for our lives, this is a huge victory. But the thinking

Careful what you wish for.

behind direct democracy does not propose putting power back in our hands on any more than a symbolic, formalistic level, because for self-government to work, power must remain centralized, alienated.

We can blame democracy and its naïve proponents for selling out this stillborn revolution, for failing to realize, after so many similar failures before them, that revolution is never pragmatic or cautious, that it must be carried beyond our horizons into the country of the unpredictable, the uncertain, the furthest bounds of our imagination, or it will die.

But we were not passive spectators to this failure. I think that on the whole, we—here I simply refer to myself and the friends I was in closest contact with in those days—quickly learned how to keep would-be politicians from taking over or centralizing the new assemblies. Or in the case of the Plaça Catalunya assembly, which quickly became too massive to function in an empowering way, we learned how to make its failings evident and how to draw out the potential of other spaces of organization and encounter. Often, this meant opposing the model of the centralized assembly based on unitary

May 21, 2011: Even if they gather to protest the elections, they will just be recruits for another party if they don't immediately begin solving their problems directly.

decision-making with our own model based on difference, on plurality, on multiple pathways of decision-making, and on total freedom of action, meaning that anyone could do what they wanted without permission from an assembly, as long as we cultivated mutual respect so that the inevitable conflicts between the different currents of activity were constructive rather than fatal.

What we did not learn how to do, I now see in hindsight, was to launch proposals that a large part of the assembly could get excited by and participate in; proposals arising from a radical analysis; proposals for solutions to austerity based in direct action and the immediate self-organization of our needs, outside and against the impositions of capitalism.

As the aforementioned text argues—true, it is not our responsibility as anarchists to come up with solutions for the rest of society, but if we ourselves are not capable of figuring out how to use heterogeneous assemblies to advance anti-authoritarian projects based on mutual aid in response to people's real needs, how can we expect anyone else to do so?

It is in this sense that the assemblies ended up being useless. No one dared take the step of using them to fulfill our collective needs. Capitalism and democratic government were waiting, as always, to step in and offer their own solutions.

This failure could be the subject for an entire book, or more appropriately, for a collective learning process involving thousands of dreamers and revolutionaries and spanning generations. In conclusion, as a simple gesture to point out other ways forward from this impasse, I will mention two components I found lacking: imagination and skills.

Imagination. The capacity to create imaginaries: visions of other worlds in which our desires and projections can reside, or even thrive, at times when capitalism permits no autonomous space in which communal relations might develop. It is no coincidence that today's revolutionary movements lack imaginaries of other worlds, nor that a great part of capitalist production supplants imagination among its consumers, offering imaginaries that become more elaborate every day, more visually stimulating, more interactive, so that people no longer have to imagine anything for themselves because a thousand worlds and fantasies already come prepackaged. All the old fantasies that used to set us dreaming have now been fixed in Hollywood productions, with convincing actors, fully depicted terrains, and emotive soundtracks. Nothing is left for us to recreate, only to consume.

In the current marketplace of ideas, it seems that the only imaginaries that describe our future are apocalypses or the science fiction colonization of outer space. The latter is the final frontier for capitalist expansion, now that this planet is rapidly getting used up, and the former is the only alternative capitalism is willing to concede outside of its dominion. We are being encouraged to imagine ourselves in the only worlds that can be conceived from within the capitalist perspective.

The revolutionaries of a hundred years ago continuously dreamed and schemed of a world without the State and without capitalism. Some of them made the mistake of turning their dreams into blueprints, dogmatic guidelines that in practice functioned as yardsticks by which to measure deviance. But today we face a much greater problem: the absence of revolutionary imaginaries and the near total atrophy of the imagination in ourselves and in the rest of society. And the imagination is the most revolutionary organ in our collective social body, because it is the only one capable of creating new worlds, of travelling outside capitalism and state authority, of enabling us to surpass the limits of insurrection that have become so evident in these last years.

Today, I know very few people who can imagine what anarchy might look like. The uncertainty is not the problem. As I hinted earlier, uncertainty is one of the fundamentals of chaotic organization, and it is only the authoritarian neurosis of states that obliges us to impose certainty on an ever-shifting reality. The problem, rather, is that this lack of imagination constitutes a disconnection from the world. A vital part of ourselves is no longer there, as it used to be, on the cusp of the horizon, on the threshold between dark and light, discerning, modulating, and greeting each new character that comes into our lives. The world of domination no longer has to contend with our Worlds Turned Upside Down; the various forms of heaven and reward promised by the authorities no longer have to bear the ridicule of our Big Rock Candy Mountains; the great shadows cast by the structures of control no longer contain a thousand possibilities of all the things we could build upon their ruins—now they are only shadows, empty and obscure.

Our prospects, however, are not irremediably bleak. Imagination can always be renewed and reinvigorated, though we must emphasize the radical importance of this work if people are once more to create, share, and discuss new possible worlds or profound transformations of this one. I would argue that this task is even more important than counter-information.

Someone who desires revolution can always educate herself, but someone who cannot even conceive a transformation will be impervious to the best-documented arguments.

Skills. Complementary to our lack of imagination is a lack of skills, though not so complete as the former. Since World War II, deskilling has been an essential feature of capitalism. The skills we need to survive in the capitalist marketplace are completely redundant, utterly useless for survival in any other mode. Without the skills to build, to heal, to fix, to transform, to feed, mutual aid and self-organization cannot be anything more than superficial, hollow slogans. What are we organizing? Just another meeting, another protest? What sort of aid are we mutualizing? Sharing our misery, sharing the garbage that capitalism hasn't yet figured out how to commercialize?

Fortunately, some people still know how to heal, how to tend, how to feed, how to build, and more people are starting to learn. Yet on the whole, these are not treated as revolutionary activities, nor are they deployed in a revolutionary way. Anyone can learn natural therapies or gardening and turn it into a business, and capitalism will happily oblige such a limited reskilling—as long as there are enough wealthy consumers to serve as patrons.

It is only when these skills are put at the service of a revolutionary imagination and a collective antagonism towards the dominant institutions that the possibility of creating a new world arises. Simultaneously, we must let our imaginaries change and grow as they come in contact with our constructive skills and the antagonism we cultivate. And the practices of negation, sabotage, and collective self-defense that have been learned in that space of antagonism must be put at the service of our constructive projects and our imaginaries, rather than being mistaken for the only serious element of struggle.

The regeneration of democracy, here and elsewhere, has given a new lease on life to the structures of domination that so many people were losing faith in. Grim futures loom, and if anything we are only getting further away from any possibility of revolution. But the chaotic reality of the universe offers us

Remember how it came to this.

a promise: nothing is predictable, no future is written, and the most rigid structures are broken, ridiculed, and forgotten in the wild, rushing river of time.

Seemingly impervious orders crumble and new forms of life emerge. We have every reason to learn from our mistakes, renew our conviction in the theories that events have confirmed, and once again offer an invitation to any who would partake in this dreamer's quest for total freedom. The easy solutions and false promises offered by the self-styled pragmatists—some of them sincere, others hungering for power—will only lead us into a defeat that we have suffered too many times before. People will learn to recognize this, if we don't let the memory fade.

Destination Anarchy! Every Step Is an Obstacle

From Syntagma Square to Syriza

Tasos Sagris, VOID NETWORK *www.voidnetwork.gr*

I find myself in the courtyard of the School of Fine Arts in Athens, Greece. It's May 25, 2011, a hot summer day. A five-day anarchist and anti-authoritarian festival starts in six hours and I am scrambling to prepare all the small details I have in mind. I'm working alone.

I walk across the campus to bring an electrician from one stage to the other.

In Spain, people have been on the streets for ten days, after 75 years of silence. They are sending us signals of revolt, bringing the flame of liberation from the Arab countries to European land. We are just setting up for our festival: sound systems for three stages and two areas for public discussions and lectures; there is a theater stage, a book fair area, and workshop areas. We are about 30 people from two small groups constructing an area for 12,000 people. We are acting like the ancient Spartans, espousing totally paranoid ideas about the limitless abilities of a small group of determined fighters.

The mind is a spaceship; people have traveled to other planets during the summer nights for thousands of years now.

May 26, 2011: The second day of protest in Syntagma Square.

As I prepare for the festival, I think to myself how we are on our way to anarchy. Sometimes it seems far away; sometimes it is suddenly all around us.

This same afternoon, there is an assembly behind the Acropolis for people hoping to bring the flame from Spain to Greece. For a year now, a small weekly anarchist assembly has met in Syntagma Square in front of the Parliament to talk about the economic crisis. At the new assembly this afternoon, people decide to go and camp in Syntagma following the calls for action coming from Tunisia, Egypt, and Spain. They publish a call for others to join them.

We can do an incredible amount of logistical work to prepare a space for people, but if the spirit of revolt draws them somewhere else, the important thing is to be there! We can spend our whole lives building a theoretical argument or an ideological position or an infrastructure for the movement—but when a revolt is taking place, we have to be ready to abandon what keeps us apart and find a way to meet each other, to exchange ideas and revolutionary practices with those in rebellion.

What appeared that day in May 2011 was a tropical storm, an ocean arising in front of our eyes, vast and wild. Fully 100,000 people gathered suddenly around the parliament, shouting

May 29, 2011: The encampment in Syntagma Square.

the classic anarchist slogan against democracy, "We Want to Burn, We Want to Burn the Parliament, this Bordello!" Nobody was at the festival for the afternoon lectures; everybody was at Syntagma. More than 8000 people arrived late at night for the concerts and the techno-trance stage. The crowd was in a frenzy, sharing an unfamiliar and wild enthusiasm.

We went to camp at Syntagma with Void Network. We announced this in the weekly anarchist assembly "For the Self-Organization of Society," which we had participated in for three years already. Some of the groups refused to come to Syntagma—they called it petit bourgeois and kept their distance, just watching. Other anarchist, autonomous, and anti-authoritarian groups stayed at Syntagma all summer. We stayed there too, spreading anarchist ideas and practices among countless desperate people, participating in the organization of the Athens General Assembly to guarantee that everyone would have an equal opportunity to express himself or herself, to ensure that no political party or ultra-left group could manipulate the decisions, to keep leftists from taking over the movement.

Other groups came only for the three days of riots. The riots were vast—a tropical storm crashing against the police and the parliament. In the middle of financial collapse, in the middle of inhuman austerity measures, unemployment, and state repression . . . this was one of the best summers of my life.

When the Greek government signed a contract with the IMF and Central European Bank in 2010, agreeing to austerity measures, it gave everyone the chance to see how global economic interests control representative democracy. People felt betrayed by politicians they had believed in for 40 years, politicians they had put in parliament to represent their interests. Furious, they imagined burning down the Parliament; many of them even tried to. Metal bars and 24/7 riot police protected the Parliament for three years, representing the final obstacle between the people and the economic interests that govern our lives.

The collapse of faith in representation was also a kind of emancipation. The obedient victims of superior logic and common sense shook free of the leadership of the politicians and the manipulation of the journalists. The unions and parties lost their influence. New forms of collective intelligence and liberation arose in place of the old identities. Wild strikes took place after decades of apathy and obedience among what we call the general public, millions of people took part in wild riots—shouting first against themselves for believing in the politicians for so many years, and then against the politicians.

The people took a step. This is what happened during the summer of 2011 in Greece and many other countries.

I find myself in my mother's house. It is June 2011. A 65-year-old social democrat, she wonders why people didn't succeed in storming the parliament yet during the days they have been encircling it. She is afraid to go out in the streets because of the tear gas, but she always asks me, "Maybe I could come also to the camp during the daytime?" My uncle and my aunt are also there, members of the Socialist Party (PASOK) since it was

June 5, 2011: The encampment in Syntagma Square.

established in 1973; now it is governing the country. My aunt is 62. With her eyes shining, she describes how last night the limousine of a famous minister of PASOK passed her outside the Parliament. She punched the back of the limousine, then ran behind it with other people to smash its windows and punch the minister. She feels liberation—she feels free! *She took a step . . .*

But were the assemblies that took place in Syntagma liberating, in the end? Or were they "directly democratic" in a way that provided the leftist party of Syriza and the fascist party of Golden Dawn with huge numbers of new adherents, for different but fundamentally similar reasons?

People expressed themselves through the assemblies all around the country. Common people who had never taken part in any kind of public event spoke openly about their deepest fears and their most precious desires, in front of thousands upon thousands of people, with megaphones to guarantee that everyone could hear their voices clearly. It was like some kind of group therapy, a catharsis in which they shook off the delusions of the past, a leap into public space, an expedition into the vast possibilities of shared social power. It was a wonderful

June 15, 2011: Fighting against nationalists at Syntagma Square.

summer when everyone was always out in the streets talking with everyone about everything.

And then democracy was re-established.

Most of the anarchists were absent, anyway, committing their biggest political mistake so far this century. In any case, we do not yet have answers for most of the problems our societies face. We know very well what is wrong with the ideas of our enemies in the parliament and the stock exchange, but our worst enemy is our own inability to bring our ideals from the clouds of anarchism down to the rough and dirty ground of anarchy.

Under these circumstances, with no other concrete options, people felt obliged—or forced—to choose between the party of social control offering them a totalitarian leader for a father figure, or the social-democratic party promising them free schools, hospitals, and some amount of protection from the wild neoliberal sharks that govern this world.

And so, after speaking in the assemblies, after participating in "direct" democracy, people got in line once again to vote, to reaffirm the democracy of the state. Every step you take towards freedom becomes an obstacle to going further. Democracy itself is an obstacle.

The democracy of our times, the highest achievement of bourgeois civilization, has built-in properties that go all the way back to its origins here in Athens thousands of years ago.

The Founding Fathers of every nation imagined themselves as the governors of uneducated savages, perverted masses of poor people ready to commit all kinds of crimes as soon as they were not controlled. Democracy was constructed by people with a political and economic interest in keeping the masses under control by means of words rather than the sword (and with the sword whenever words are not enough). Representative democracy is a system of mind control offering a pseudo-reality of freedom in which you cannot have any serious influence over the fundamental decisions about your life.

The Founding Fathers of democracy—like all fathers, perhaps—feared the critical thinking of their children. They set up a system intended to keep people stupid: we remain in a childish state of mind, participating in obligatory social structures in which we cannot realize the totality of our capabilities and desires. There is no need to know the exact details of the decisions that determine your life; you just have to vote for whichever politician you prefer to govern your life. This system fosters corruption, as the leaders drain the resources of the community, and keeps people apathetic. Nobody gives a damn about your opinion; you are just one statistic among millions. You are not supposed to speak out; you are supposed to remain silent as your governors speak. You are there to applaud. Throughout your entire political life, you are absent, represented.

Democracy keeps you afraid, afraid of the enemies of democracy that have hidden within your tribe, your democratic community, your nation. Democracy creates borders in your life and you are drafted to protect those borders with your own body. The borders are imaginary, just social constructs, but your dead body on the battleground is real. Democracy excludes the rest of humanity from your community and it prepares an army, including you, to kill all the excluded ones. And if you refuse to kill for the sake of democracy, you too will be excluded.

June 15, 2011: Riot police line up at Syntagma Square behind a banner reading "DIRECT DEMOCRACY."

This system has an amazing ability to reproduce itself. It produces schools, hospitals, theaters, kindergartens, military camps, university campuses, galleries, museums, amusement parks. You can spend your whole life inside those institutions, and if you try to escape from them, you will probably end up in a homeless shelter, a jail, or a psychiatric clinic (all of which are also democratic institutions). The consequence of this resilience is that democracy is unable to surpass itself, to evolve into something different, in the same way that the Soviet Union never arrived at the communist paradise.

Statutes and politicians and even means of governing may be replaced, but democracy is always the same oligarchic system, aristocratic in its core. Democracy is always searching, through elections and business contracts and nepotism, for the best ones to perpetuate it.

This is nothing new. Democracy is a conservative tribal method by which certain ancient Greek tribes reproduced themselves. It will never allow you to become different until you escape from the tribe. Today, when the capitalist market and the democratic state exert total control all around the world, there is no other way to escape democracy except to destroy it.

Even knowing all of this, some people defend democracy. They want to find a form of democracy that doesn't end up in oligarchy, just like the 21st century communists who are searching for communist systems that don't lead to totalitarianism. But the Founding Fathers of all nations loom over democrats of all stripes, looking on approvingly as normality reasserts itself—the same conditions of exploitation, new faces in the same old positions of authority.

This world will never change as long as we are afraid to cut the roots of this order. Democracy is the final alternative for all who are afraid to step into the unknown territory of their own desires, their own power. Likewise, the demand for "real" democracy is the last way for social movements to legitimize themselves in the supposed "social sphere" (and to try to avoid being criminalized). Just as it is the final step, democracy is also the final obstacle to new possibilities arising in social movements.

Could any form of democracy save us from democracy?

Direct democracy offers us an alternative way to govern our lives. But is this really what we need? Do we want to reproduce the limits of the old world on a smaller scale? Do we want the general assembly to decide our lives? Or do we want to expand our lives towards some new form of self-determination?

When I take part in the assembly of Void Network, I have to take into account the needs and interests of all my comrades,

June 28, 2011: Nationalist flags replace the banner demanding direct democracy in Syntagma Square.

and our group has to take into account the needs and desires of the greatest possible number of people in this world. If we do not take care of each other, there can be no Void Network, and if we do not take care of the people outside our group, there will be no connection between us and the world. There is no general assembly that could know better than we do how we should make the most of our abilities to benefit the people around us. This is the difference between an affinity group, which produces a collective and expansive power, and a democratic assembly, which concentrates power in an institutional space

June 29, 2011: Greek riot police, the new hoplites* imposing democracy on the exploited and excluded.

distinct from our lives and relationships, alienating us from ourselves and each other.

Direct democracy is supposed to get rid of the apathy produced by representation, since it appears as a "participatory" form of democracy. But is the idea that we will have an assembly of millions of people? Would such an assembly really be capable of offering us freedom and equality? Each of us would just feel like a statistic in it as we waited for days for our turn to speak. On the other hand, if we reduce that form to the miniscule level of a neighborhood assembly, don't we trap ourselves in a microcosm like oversized ants?

Any kind of "direct democracy" reproduces the same conditions as representative democracy, just on a smaller scale. The

---

* Hoplites—armored infantrymen fighting shoulder to shoulder in phalanxes—constituted the main force of the citizen militias that defended Greek city-states in the era when democracy emerged. According to some theories, their importance in military matters gave them enough leverage to compel the aristocratic class to grant them political rights.

majority suppresses the minority, driving them into apathy. Often, you don't even try to express your opinion, as you know you will have no chance to put it into practice. Often, you are afraid to speak, as you know that you will be humiliated by the majority. Homogeneity is the ultimate imperative of any democratic procedure, "direct" or representational—a homogeneity that ends up as two final opinions (the majority and minority), losing the vast richness of human intelligence and sensibility, erasing all the complexity and diversity of human needs and desires.

This is why even directly democratic assemblies can end up deciding to carry out inhuman genocides, like the one ancient Athens inflicted upon Mylos in 416 BC. Excluded people have been enslaved and raped as a result of direct democratic decisions. Direct democracy is "members only." Because it is smaller, it excludes even more people than representative democracy—producing isolated bubbles that fight each other like the city-states of ancient Greece. Everybody is an outsider, a foreigner, a possible enemy; that's why the community has to build armies to defend itself and you have to die to protect the opinion of the majority even if you disagree with it. Whoever will not go along with the decision must be punished—like Socrates, the world-famous victim of democracy, and countless others. The charismatic leaders find the best possible direct connection with their followers, and the mechanisms for manipulating public opinion work directly better than ever!

Direct democracy will never liberate us from democracy.

Months later, I find myself at my mother's house again. It is early in September 2011, a few days before Occupy Wall Street begins. I am sending out emails to comrades in the USA, urging them to expand the encampments all over the states, to spread anarchist ideas and methodologies in the Occupy movement assemblies.

My uncle is also there. As I am looking at my screen, he says to me, "We decided now to move"—I look up at him—"away from PASOK, to try the European communist party of SYRIZA." I feel terror, because I know that when he says, "We decided," he speaks for about two million people. It's as if he knows them all individually—they are the betrayed followers of PASOK, and he was in the social-democrat party from the first day to the last. Syriza had only 4% of the votes just one day ago. I am looking at him, seeing two million zombies walk just a few steps from one party to another. I want to shout, "YOU HAVE TO MOVE FURTHER! EVERY STEP IS A NEW OBSTACLE! YOU CAN'T STOP THERE . . ."

Anarchists have a lot to do before we can speak to this kind of person. They are the realists, these people who understand politics as the management of reality.

I imagine history as a beautiful girl: she smiles, and riots explode in Athens. I see history departing from Athens after staying a long time in my city, now that delusional hopes of change through the parliament have been planted once more in people's minds.

Three and a half years later, in 2015, the streets are still silent as the Euro-communists of SYRIZA win the elections with just one word for a campaign slogan: HOPE. (The last thing left in Pandora's box.) To me, it seems more like DESPERATION.

One of the first decisions the new government of Syriza makes is to remove the protective metal bars and riot police from around the Parliament. The Parliament is safe once more. Within a few months of the election, SYRIZA betrays all of its promises to the Greek people, caving in to all the austerity policies demanded by the European Union.

It's an old, old story, repeated yet again. Democracy never changes. It just reforms and reproduces itself.

Every step is a new obstacle. 2600 years ago in Greece and two centuries ago in Europe the struggle for democracy promised to liberate the poverty-stricken masses from their misery. A few years later, they found themselves in exactly the same conditions—in eternal war with all possible outsiders, now with the right to vote for their rulers. Christianity and Islam attracted millions of poor people with promises of social justice

Defending a space of freedom in Syntagma Square.

and eternal love; a few years later, they became ideological tools for massive genocides all around the world, absolute enemies of human emancipation and obstacles to the arising of human spirituality. The Communist Party, proclaimed to be the voice of all those without voices, became the worst enemy of freedom of expression. Anarchists became ministers and governors in the Spanish revolution—and the CNT, the great organization for the liberation of the workers, organized them to work at the factories for their whole lives until their heroic deaths. We might sacrifice our lives to liberate ourselves from the old world's prisons only to find ourselves locked inside a new high-quality jail.

Anarcho-communism, an emancipatory vision that we all share in Void Network, is an old vision of a world without money and without borders. But it needs to be updated for the 21st century—otherwise, it will remain in our minds like a mythological ghost, another obstacle. If we want a world without money, this means we have to transform labor into open-source creativity, to turn workplaces into beautiful parks of voluntary creative participation in a global web that freely distributes all material and mental production. Life has to be organized around the production of desires and the enjoyment of needs. If we want a world without borders, that means a world without foreigners—so you will not be a "stranger" anywhere in the world at any moment of your life. We have to transform societies into open and inclusive communities connected in a global network, so that everyone can be welcome and useful anywhere and anytime on this planet, not divided into isolated, xenophobic groups. We have to open "ourselves" to the difference of all the "others."

In the eight decades since the collapse of the Spanish Revolution, anarchists have avoided offering solid plans for anarchist revolution on this scale. Meanwhile, during those years, capitalism has evolved to levels that the revolutionaries of late 19th century could not have imagined. Global capitalism is here, global anarchism is not.

The only possible way that an anarchist revolution could happen is on a planetary scale—not on a local scale, not on isolated islands. Even if it will take 200 years for an anarchist revolution to extend to every corner of this world, this has to be envisioned, planned, and realized.

If we reduce the scale of our organizational structures to local neighborhood assemblies or tiny eco-communities, we will find ourselves dealing with problems that pass through our small community the way that huge ocean waves pass over a small fishing boat. Neo-totalitarianism will never leave us alone in alternative-lifestyle bubbles (though neoliberalism might sell vacations in eco-paradises to the rich). We cannot separate ourselves from the suffering of this world.

On the other hand, if we permit old or new forms of authoritarian mass structures to oblige us to embrace their notions of efficiency and practicality, we will end up in the belly of a new bureaucratic monster. We need a global network of communities in struggle, a network of millions of flexible groups ready to fight against totalitarianism, to create public liberated zones, to defend them against their enemies and connect them in a revolutionary wave of global social emancipation—and to do all this without central control.

In 1964, Marshall McLuhan wrote in his book *Understanding Media: The Extensions of Man* that

> The Greeks had the notion of a consensus or a faculty of "common sense" that translated each sense into each other sense, and conferred consciousness on man. Today, when we have extended all parts of our bodies and senses by technology, we are haunted by the need for an outer consensus of technology and experience that would raise our communal lives to the level of a worldwide consensus. When we have achieved a worldwide fragmentation, it is not unnatural to think about a worldwide integration. Such a universality of conscious being for mankind was dreamt of by Dante, who believed that men would remain mere broken fragments until they should be united in an inclusive consciousness.

Could anarchy—total freedom, absolute social and economic equality, and global fellowship—offer an inclusive consciousness to a fragmented humanity for the 21st century?

It is not simple even to begin thinking about it. And if we want a vision of emancipation that is created socially and collectively, we have to avoid simplistic solutions and the leadership of specific individuals. For example, Karl Marx was a very smart man, but Marxism is an obstacle for free thinking.

We are fighting against the state and capitalism to open passages—practices, strategies, and methodologies—that lead to total freedom, social equality, mutual aid, and self-determination. We have to find a way to connect with the many, in order that together we may transform the conditions that produce our reality. Against homogeneity, we have to foster diversity; against certitude, we have to make space for all truths; against exclusion, we want to empower the stranger, the queer, the old, the young, the freak, the unknown; against borders, we want to live openheartedly; against atomization, to care for others, to learn from each other, to carry out our great plans and achieve our ultimate goals. Otherwise, established political authority and economic interests will reassert themselves in endless variations on the same conditions. This world will never change until we dare to *live free,* to *share everything,* to *spread anarchy!*

Destination:
Anarchy.
Every
step
is an
obstacle.

Democracy versus Autonomy in the Occupy Movement

The story goes that the very first gathering to plan Occupy Wall Street began as an old-fashioned top-down rally with speakers droning on—until a Greek anarchist interrupted and demanded that they hold a proper horizontal assembly instead.* She and some of the younger people in attendance sat down in a circle on the other side of the plaza and began holding a meeting using consensus process. One by one, more people trickled over from the audience that had been listening to speakers and joined the circle. It was August 2, 2011.

Here, in the origin myth of the Occupy Movement, we encounter the fundamental ambiguity in its relationship to organization. We can understand this shift to consensus process as the adoption of a more inclusive and therefore more legitimate democratic model, anticipating later claims that the general assemblies of Occupy represented real democracy in action. Or we can focus on the decision to withdraw from the initial rally, seeing it as a gesture in favor of voluntary association. Over the following year, this internal tension erupted repeatedly, pitting democrats determined to demonstrate a new form of governance against anarchists intent upon asserting the primacy of autonomy.

Though David Graeber† encouraged participants to regard consensus as a set of principles rather than rules, both the proponents of consensus process and its authoritarian opponents persisted in treating it as a formal means of government—while anarchists who shared Graeber's framework found themselves outside the consensus reality of their fellow Occupiers. The movement's failure to reach consensus about the meaning of consensus itself culminated with ugly attacks in which the pundits Rebecca Solnit and Chris Hedges attempted to brand anarchist participants as violent thugs.‡

* Sean Captain's "The Inside Story of Occupy Wall Street" credits Georgia Sagri—the sister of the primary author of the preceding chapter.

† For example, in "Some Remarks on Consensus."

‡ See "Throwing Out the Master's Tools and Building a Better House: Thoughts on the Importance of Nonviolence in the Occupy Revolution" and "The Cancer in Occupy"; see also our response, "The Illegitimacy of Violence, the Violence of Legitimacy."

How did that play out in the hinterlands, where small-town Occupy groups took up the decision-making practices of Occupy Wall Street? Let's shift from New York City to a small town in Middle America to find out.

I live in a town with a population of less than 100,000. We have a university, a sizeable part of the population engaged in service sector work that barely pays the bills, and a greater number of active anarchists than most towns this size.

A decade and a half ago, I participated in the so-called "anti-globalization movement," so dubbed by corporate journalists who had apparently been instructed not to print the word anti-capitalist. Beginning with a groundswell of local initiatives, it culminated in a string of massive riots at international trade summits including the World Trade Organization summit in Seattle in November 1999, the International Monetary Fund and World Bank meetings in Washington, DC in April 2000 and Prague in September 2000, the summit to plan the Free Trade Area of the Americas in Quebec City in April, 2001, and the G8 summit in Genoa in July 2001.

Although I had been an anarchist for some years already, I learned to use consensus process in the course of those demonstrations. Like many other participants, I believed that this form of decision-making pointed the way to a world without government or capitalism. We cherished the seemingly quixotic dream that one day this obscure subcultural decision-making process might spread to the population at large.

Ten years later, in September 2011, I visited the Occupy Wall Street encampment at Zuccotti Park. It had only existed for two weeks, yet it had already developed its political culture: daily assemblies, "mic check," consensus process. This was all familiar to me from my anti-globalization days, though most people there clearly did not share that background.

I heard a lot of legalistic and reformist rhetoric in the course of my brief visit. At the same time, this was what we had dreamed of: our organizational structures and decision-making practices spreading outside our milieu. Could the practices themselves instill the political values that had originally inspired us to employ them? Some of my comrades had argued that directly democratic models could help to radicalize people who were not yet ready for the likes of anarchism. The following months put that theory to the test.

Two weeks after my visit to Manhattan, I was back in my hometown in Middle America, attending our Occupy group's second assembly. We had gathered in the central plaza on the main thoroughfare. A hundred people from a wide range of backgrounds and political perspectives were debating whether to establish an encampment of our own.

It's not easy for a crowd arbitrarily convened through an open invitation on Facebook to make a decision together. Some people were arguing against establishing an occupation

WANT TO TALK   **DIRECT RESPONSE**   **CLARIFY**

POINT OF ORDER   **OPPOSE**   **BLOCK**

AGREE   **DON'T AGREE**

immediately; they said that the police would just evict us, and insisted that we should apply for a permit first.

Yet in the nearest city, occupiers had applied for a permit but were only granted one lasting a few hours. Everyone who remained after it expired was arrested. A few of us thought it better to go forward without permission than to embolden the authorities to believe we would comply with whatever was convenient for them.

A different facilitator would have let the debate remain abstract indefinitely, effectively quashing the possibility of an occupation in the name of consensus. But ours cut right to the chase: "Raise your hand if you want to camp out here to-night." A few hands went hesitantly up. "Looks like five . . . six, seven . . . OK, let's split into two groups: those who want to occupy, and everyone else. We'll reconvene in ten minutes."

At first there were only a half dozen of us meeting on the occupiers' side of the plaza, but after we took the first step, others drifted over. Ten minutes later, there were twenty-four of us—and that night dozens of people camped out in the Plaza. I stayed up all night waiting for the police to raid, but they never showed up. We'd won the first round, expanding what everyone imagined to be possible—and we owed it to people taking the initiative autonomously, not to everyone reaching consensus.

Our occupation was a success. Over the first few weeks, scores of people met and got to know each other through frequent demonstrations, logistical work, and nights of impassioned discussion.

The nightly assemblies served as a space to become better acquainted politically. First, we heard a wide range of testimonials about why people were there. These ranged from boring to fascinating, but they died out swiftly once the business of making decisions via assemblies got underway. Next, we weathered lengthy debates about whether there should be a nonviolence policy, with nonviolence serving as a code word for legalistic obedience. Thanks to the participation of many

anarchists, this discussion was split pretty much down the middle, and no consensus was ever reached. If nothing else, it enabled many occupiers who had never been part of a movement like this to hear arguments from both sides of the issue.

It was interesting to watch so many people go through such a rapid political evolution. I enjoyed the debates, the drama of watching middle-class liberals struggle to converse on an equal footing with anarchists and other angry poor people.

On the other hand, the assemblies were ineffective as a way to make decisions. After weeks of grueling daily sessions, we gave up entirely on formulating a mission statement about our basic goals, consensus having been repeatedly blocked by a lone right-wing libertarian contrarian. Some people managed to push a couple small demonstrations through the consensus process, but these attracted few participants. The assembly's stamp of approval did not correlate with people actually investing themselves; the momentum to make an effort succeed was determined elsewhere.

While the nightly assemblies helped us get to know each other politically, if you wanted to get to know people personally, you had to spend more time at the encampment. Standing night watch, facing off with drunk college students and other reactionaries, I became acquainted with many of the occupiers who had first arrived as disconnected individuals. It was those connections that gave us cause to be invested in each other's efforts over the following months.

Unexpectedly, the liberals were among those most invested in the protocol of consensus process, even though most of them had learned it from us. However unfamiliar it was, they found it reassuring that there was a proper way of doing things. This emphasis on protocol created rifts with the actual inhabitants of the encampment, many of whom felt ill at ease communicating in such a formal structure; that class divide proved to be a more fundamental conflict than any political disagreement. From the perspective of the liberals, there was a democratic assembly in which anyone could participate, and those who did not attend or speak up could not complain about the decisions made there. From the vantage point of those who lived in the camp, the liberals showed up for an hour or two every couple days, expecting to be able to dictate decisions to people who were in the camp twenty-four hours a day. Usually, they didn't even stick around to implement them.

When I left town to visit other Occupy groups or talked with friends across the country, they all reported something similar. The conflict between the general assembly and the encampment was practically universal. It expressed the most fundamental tensions within the movement.

As one of the few participants who had already been familiar with consensus process yet spent considerable time in the camp outside the assemblies, I could see both sides. I tried to explain to the liberals who only showed up for the assemblies—the ones who understood Occupy as a political project rather than a social space—that there were already functioning decision-making processes at work in the encampment, however informal those might be. If they wanted to establish better relations with the residents of the encampment, I argued, they should take those processes seriously and try to participate in them, too.

After the first few weeks, the flow of new participants slowed. We were becoming a known quantity. Consequently,

we began to lose our leverage on the authorities and our hold on the popular imagination. Meanwhile, it was getting colder out, and winter was on the way. Based on our experience attempting to formulate a mission statement or call for demonstrations, it seemed clear that if there was to be a next step, it would have to be determined outside the general assemblies.

I got together with some friends I had known and trusted for a long time—the same group that had called for Occupy in our town in the first place. We discussed whether to occupy a vast empty building a few blocks from the plaza. Most of us thought it was impossible, but a few fanatics insisted it could be done. We decided that if they could get us inside, we would try to hold onto it. But the plan had to be a secret until we were in, so the police couldn't stop us.

The building occupation was a success. Over a hundred people flooded into the building, setting up a kitchen, a reading library, and sleeping quarters. A band performed, followed by a dance party. That night, dozens of people slept in the building rather

than at the plaza, relieved to be out of the cold. Once again, I stood watch all night, waiting for the police. The stakes were higher this time, but they still didn't show up. Spirits were high: once again, we had expanded the space of possibility.

The following afternoon, as we continued cleaning and repairing the building, a rumor circulated that the police were preparing a raid. Several dozen of us gathered for an impromptu meeting. It struck me how different the atmosphere was from our usual general assemblies. There were no bureaucratic formalities, no deadlocks over minutia. No one droned on just to hear himself speak or stared off listlessly. There was no grandstanding or chiding each other about protocol.

Perhaps that was because here, there was nothing abstract about the issues at hand. Just by being present, we were putting our bodies on the line. We were discussing real choices that would have immediate consequences for all of us. We didn't need a facilitator to listen to each other or stay on topic. With our freedom at stake, we had every reason to work well together.

The day after the raid, a huge crowd gathered at the original encampment for a contentious general assembly—the biggest and most energetic our town witnessed throughout the entire sequence of Occupy. Our decision to occupy the building, arrived at outside the general assembly, had ironically made the general assembly irresistible to everyone. Some people were inspired by the building occupation and our response to the police raid; others, who assumed the general assembly to be the governing body of the movement, were outraged that we had bypassed it; still others, who had not been interested in Occupy until now, came to engage with us because they could see we were capable of making a big impact. Even if they were only there to argue that we should "be peaceful" and obey the law, we hoped that entering that space of dialogue might expand their sense of what was possible, too.

So the assembly benefitted from the building occupation, whether or not people approved of it. But ironically, they only came because of the power we had expressed by acting on our own, without its stamp of approval. It was this power that they sought to access through the assembly—some to increase it, some to command it, some to tame it. In fact, the power didn't reside in the assembly as a decision-making space, but in the people who came to it and the connections they forged there.

Over the following week, people inspired by the building occupations in Oakland and our little town occupied buildings in St. Louis, Washington, DC, and Seattle. This new wave of actions pushed the Occupy movement from symbolic protests towards directly challenging the sanctity of capitalist notions of property. Our town saw its biggest unpermitted demonstrations in years.

Months later, I compared notes with comrades around the country about how this mass experiment in consensus process had turned out. Everywhere, there had been the same conflicts, as some people who saw the assemblies as the legitimate space of decision-making criticized those who propelled the movement forward for acting autonomously. Even in Oakland, famously the most confrontational encampment in the country, almost everything that gave it its character never passed through the general assembly. They experienced the same controversies we did, writ large. In a photograph taken after the riots with which occupiers retaliated against the eviction of their encampment, someone has written on a broken window, "This act of vandalism was NOT authorized by the GA," as if the GA were a governmental body, answerable for its subjects and therefore entitled to legitimize or delegitimize their actions.

That shows a profound misunderstanding of what consensus procedure is good for. Like any tool, power flows from us to it, not the other way around—we can invest it with power, but using it won't necessarily make us more powerful. Every single step that made Occupy succeed in our town, from the call for the first assembly to the decision to occupy the plaza to the decision to occupy a building, was the result of an autonomous initiative. We never could have reached consensus to do any of those things in an open assembly that included anarchists, Maoists, reactionary poor people, middle-class liberals, police infiltrators, people with mental health issues, aspiring politicians, and whoever else happened to stop by.

The assemblies were essential as a space where we could intersect and exchange proposals, creating new affinities and building a sense of our collective power. But we don't need a more participatory—and therefore even more inefficient and invasive—form of government. We need the ability to act freely as we see fit, the common sense to coexist with others wherever possible, and the courage to stand up for ourselves whenever there are real conflicts.

As the Occupy movement was dying down, the faction that was most invested in legalism and protocol called for a National Gathering in Philadelphia on July 4, 2012, at which to "collectively craft a Vision of a Democratic Future." Barely 500 people showed from around the country, a tiny fraction of the number that had blocked ports, occupied parks, and marched in the streets. The people, as they say, had voted with their feet.

Democratic Practices and Institutional Legitimacy in Occupy Oakland

In the process of preparing this book, we recorded a discussion with some participants in Occupy Oakland about their experiences with democratic and autonomous practices in the course of the Occupy movement. The following is comprised of excerpts from a much longer conversation.

Let's start with the role of the General Assembly in Occupy Oakland. I've heard a wide variety of contradictory perspectives about how anarchists related to it. The answers run the gamut between two poles.

At one extreme, some people argue that everything worthwhile that occurred during Occupy Oakland only took place because of the leverage anarchists had in the General Assembly. This view seems to affirm a sort of democratic centralism: centralized decision-making is legitimate and desirable, as long as anarchists are the ones calling the shots.

At the other extreme, other people argue that legitimizing the General Assembly in any way is contrary to the values of autonomy. In that view, the less that people rely on the General Assembly, the better. The problem with this position is that it offers no analysis of the role that the General Assembly played in the tremendous surge in momentum that anti-capitalist and anti-state organizing experienced in the Bay Area in 2011.

In your view, to what extent did anarchists legitimize the General Assembly of Occupy Oakland as the governing body of the movement? What were the advantages and disadvantages of this approach? And did that facilitate autonomous activity, or interfere with it?

B: One of the key functions that anarchists played in Occupy Oakland was in shaping the principles of the General Assembly, so they would not be as restrictive and narrowly democratic—you might say authoritarian—as in many other Occupy groups. The emphasis was on understanding the assembly as a forum for people to express ideas and find other people to collaborate with, and then go forward with those projects without waiting for permission.

T: In many Occupy groups, there was an idea that everything had to be approved by the general assembly. In Oakland, it was explicitly asserted that autonomous action should be coordinated outside it. Certain people were never happy about this, but that was the understanding from day one.

P: But I don't think that the support for autonomous actions was ever formally agreed on. It was just something many people asserted at the beginning. There were a few things like that that were said early on and just stuck. Another example was the refusal to let police into the encampment. There was never a vote on that.

T: That was understood from the beginning. Among the random people who showed up at first, in response to the initial call,

Occupy Oakland on day five at Oscar Grant Plaza.

the overwhelming sentiment was, "This is Oakland, and no police are allowed at this occupation."

B: When they tried to enter, people always surrounded them!

P: All those cases beg the question: was the General Assembly an anarchistic forum or a democratic forum? There was never a vote agreeing that the GA didn't have the authority to forbid certain actions: that was already assumed by the people who called for it in the first place. Yes, there was voting, there were proposals about where to occupy and what to name the occupation—but all of that was framed in an anarchistic way, not a democratic way.

B: Thinking back, I can pick out several different forms of autonomous action that were essential to Occupy Oakland. When the assembly would call for a demonstration, for example, it was understood that there were no prescribed guidelines for what kind of tactics people were allowed to employ.

So that was one way that the GA opened space for autonomous action. But it was also important that most of the day-to-day functioning of the camp was organized autonomously. There were committees, but they didn't do or determine everything. For example, when the grass was getting too muddy, one day a pathway of pallets appeared connecting the entire camp. People just took pallets from stores in Oakland and built those pathways. The GA didn't "open up space" for that to happen, it just happened.

P: In the standard political framework, there's a sort of Cartesian dualism in the separation between the "mind" of the movement and its body. On the one side, there is the political forum, like the GA in Occupy Oakland. On the other side, there is the beating heart of the movement—the kitchen, for example. The most amazing parts of Occupy were the vital, organic parts. The political forum was amazing too, but nothing compared to the lived experience of being together. There's a tendency to focus on the political theater more than what actually happens. In Occupy Oakland, they were both intertwined, and both essential.

B: In some ways, you could say that anarchists had an advantage in that space because they felt comfortable taking initiatives without waiting for institutional go-ahead, whereas other people assumed that they needed the approval of this assembly.

But there were conflicts in the General Assembly about what should be permitted, right?

B: It's true, many people put a lot of energy into combatting authoritarian proposals in the assembly—there was a modified consensus in which we had to reach 90% for a proposal to pass. A lot of what anarchists were doing in the assembly was just making sure that nothing ever passed that abridged anyone's autonomy. There were multiple attempts to pass a nonviolence resolution, for example. None of them ever passed.

Still, we spent a lot of time making sure that none of those proposals passed. And that would get pretty . . . procedural. Like, people were using phone trees to get each other out to certain assemblies: "You've gotta be here at 6:15 in time to speak." Like, stacking the list of speakers against a certain proposal. "And make sure that you talk to the facilitator beforehand to get that other proposal off the list."

P: You had to get people in the facilitation committees.

T: It was very . . . parliamentarian, you know?

B: In the 1930s, the Communist Party in the United States was famous for going to union halls and positioning one of their members in each corner. They had a name for it, even. At a certain point, in Occupy Oakland, it occurred to us that we were all sitting in the same place, and, "Well, maybe we need to spread out . . ."

So sometimes we were doing something like that. At the end of the day, I thought that was important, even though . . . it was a little weird. We put a tremendous amount of energy into trying to influence how things went in the General Assembly, in hopes that as a result, there would be fewer restrictions on activity . . .

. . . In terms of what was regarded as legitimate.

B: Yeah, exactly.

That's a little ironic, isn't it? Relying on protocol to block proposals that would centralize the authority of the assembly? I can understand it as a way to engage in necessary public debate about what should be considered acceptable and where legitimacy should reside. But to the extent to which those conclusions have legitimacy in people's minds because they received a stamp of approval from the assembly, you're winning the battle by losing the war.

In our Occupy group, we never agreed that the General Assembly would be the governing body of the movement. But once our general assembly was understood as a place where

power was wielded, one of the ways that people competed for that power was by trying to determine the protocol by which decisions would be made. The other way was by trying to use the assembly to prescribe what sort of actions should be viewed as legitimate. In those debates, we often found ourselves grounding our arguments in established precedent, even when it was basically arbitrary. And precedent is also a kind of authority.

For example, after our building occupation, when there were intense arguments about whether it was acceptable to occupy buildings, some of us cited the original Occupy Wall Street Call to Action in which they called for people to occupy buildings. We were arguing for autonomous actions by pointing to the founding documents of the Occupy movement, behaving as though autonomy was vouchsafed . . .

P: . . . by a decision that had previously been made at another assembly, in a totally different part of the country.

Exactly.

Oscar Grant Plaza during the general strike of November 2, 2011.

T: OK, first, about the General Assembly, I don't think anyone was manipulating anything. We were just utilizing it.

I mean, who set up the General Assembly? It wasn't like it was someone else's structure we were coopting. Anarchists created it, with a 90% threshold for consensus so that five people couldn't block things. Anarchists were in the kitchen, anarchists were cleaning the bathroom, anarchists were running security, anarchists were organizing the marches, anarchists were facilitating the assemblies. And we all knew each other from years of experience, so people were better positioned to make things happen than anyone else.

I'm the only person here who was on the facilitation committee. It wasn't like people were breaking the rules or anything.

B: I didn't mean there was manipulation in the sense of breaking the rules. I mean that . . . We had an agenda and we went there to push that agenda through. Being able to stack the discussions, getting people there—that was important. During the slower periods, I remember there were some days when I would just show up to the General Assembly for a vote and then leave—if it was a busy day and I was at work, I would show up just long enough to vote and go back to work.

T: As for what you're saying about the seating . . . All the liberals and pacifists would sit on the right side, and on the left side there was a smoking section right by 14th Street. That was where all the anarchists hung out. Everyone would be wearing black there and smoking. People called it the black lung bloc. And that group just constantly blocked—just blocked proposals, one after another. Sometimes that group would be 200 people, and they would just block anything that would potentially constrain action.

You're saying that was on the left? Just like in the National Assembly in France at the end of the 18th century, when the opponents of the monarchy would sit on the left side of the parliament?

T: Yeah, totally.

So, it's like . . . You think you're just in some local protest movement, but you're actually participating in struggles that are hundreds of years old, and maybe unconsciously reproducing patterns and roles from them.

T: Ugh.

Here's the question I have, then. When socialists engage in the same activity that you just described, we're critical of it. Let's say they are there from the beginning of a social movement, and they set up a decision-making space that functions according to their values, and everyone comes to rely on it the way that everyone relied on the General Assembly of Occupy Oakland. When they succeed in centralizing their structure that way, they are able to marginalize anyone who doesn't accept their leadership and their restrictions—at least, unless we are able to delegitimize the structure itself.

So in that situation—is our critique that the wrong group has achieved hegemony in that space, so it operates by the wrong values? In that case, our goal would be to see to it that people with the right values dictate what happens in the decision-making process. But that basically means trying to accomplish the same thing that the socialists are, and utilizing the same tactics. And if they outmaneuver us, then all the legitimacy invested in the space that we were competing for transfers to them.

Or do we have a different idea of how those spaces should work, in the first place, so that it's not a question of who is in control of them? In that case, we have to spread a totally different framework for how people should relate to those spaces, not just try to win the debates that take place in them.

P: To me, it came down to asserting different values, both in the assembly and outside it. That's what justified our approach, even if it's a slippery slope. There are many problems with that sort of vanguardism. But it served an anti-authoritarian purpose in protecting the movement as a whole from would-be leaders who would concentrate too much power in their hands. Sure, there were moments where people would slip into leadership positions. But the idea was to construct a format that would allow different kinds of people to come together and interact without authoritarian elements being able to dominate.

T: Whether or not this argument is legitimate, whenever anarchists participate in democratic frameworks here, the justification has always been that it was to protect the social movement from authoritarians. Like, it's OK to be sort of vanguardist in order to make sure vanguardists can't take power.

B: But if socialists had been doing the same thing in the assembly, it's true, we would have accused them of vanguardism, right? I thought a lot about this. There were some people who were throwing around accusations, like, "Y'all are being Leninists."

T: "Anarcho-Leninists." We heard that a lot.

B: Here's the thing, though. If the ISO [International Socialist Organization] or the RCP [Revolutionary Communist Party] or

Whole Foods Market in downtown Oakland during the general strike.

one of these parasitic groups had succeeded in gaining that much influence, they would have had really different intentions.

For example, they seek ideological uniformity, whereas none of us necessarily share an ideology. That's important, I think. Anarchists in Occupy Oakland never shared an ideology. They shared principles, and values, and tactics, but nothing more than that. If you had sat down in the black lung bloc and asked any of us about our opinions, we would all have very different answers as to how we understand the world.

When the RCP or the ISO seek to gain control over demonstrations or movements in Oakland, their goal is to imbue them with a specific ideology. Whereas what unites us is that we are always asking how to push these movements further. I think that those are very different things.

P: I want to consider this idea of legitimacy. The general assembly was a tool that we used in a specific context. What is the point of being anarchists if we are not going to experiment with different tools? Should we throw the baby out with the bathwater every time some elements of a tool are not exactly to our liking? Being purists isn't going to get us anywhere.

A banner strung across the central intersection of downtown Oakland during the strike.

This is one of the things that has gone fairly well in the Bay Area, historically: being willing to take risks and try things that might be a little out of the ordinary for anarchists. It's a way of encountering people different from you, people who could be interested in these new ideas and ways of acting. Just because we use a tool doesn't make it legitimate—it doesn't mean saying it should have power over anyone. It's just like we can use social media while still being critical of it. We have to engage with the rest of the world, even though it isn't structured for people like us, or for people who want what we want.

Of course, the real issue comes up when we have crossed that bridge, we get to the other side, and suddenly we see that we are building a new world that has some of the same structures as the old one. And that's where I see more serious questions come up.

Murray Bookchin made the same argument for participating in local municipal elections, you know—he argued that they were tools that we could use to move towards a free society.

I'm not trying to get anarchists to be purists, but . . . some people once argued that you have to seize the apparatus of the state to dismantle it, too, and you see where that has gotten us. If the General Assembly has the right to legitimize autonomous actions, it also has the right to forbid them. If we believe that autonomous actions are legitimate whether or not they are endorsed by the General Assembly, we can use the General Assembly to make that argument, but only by treating it as a public forum rather than a decision-making body.

T: To me, the best part of all the assemblies was the discussion. Sometimes when a proposal was brought up, thirty people or forty people would speak in the comment section before the vote. And people would give amazing speeches, saying things I've never heard anyone say before. We all said things that we've never said before, especially in front of a thousand people in front of City Hall.

That was the coolest part. I've always thought, what would happen if we did all the speaking, and then skipped the vote? Like, not have any actual decision-making? I don't know if that would draw as much participation.

OK, so let's come at this from the opposite direction now, to see if we can make a case for treating the General Assembly as a governing body.

The strongest argument I have heard in favor of the role of democratic process in Occupy is that the decision calling for the general strike of November 2 only had enough force to draw tens of thousands of people into the streets because it was made by consensus in a massive, publicly recognized decision-making organ.

T: That assembly took place just after the police raided the camp for the first time. There were two thousand people there: all these people who had not participated before, who got involved because the police fractured [Iraq War veteran] Scott Olsen's skull.

The General Assembly didn't become such a contentious place until after that. That's when you started to hear proposal after proposal about whether to restrict tactics.

But can we imagine a mobilization on the scale of the general strike coming about in any other way? You were talking about how Occupy Oakland functioned as a space for people to find each other and undertake projects autonomously . . . but would November 2 have been such a success if it had just been an idea that people discussed, rather than a proposal that was officially endorsed by what was basically an executive political body?

T: Well, everyone was talking about a general strike from the beginning. After the occupation of the capitol building in Wisconsin in February 2011, you would see the idea of a general strike popping up on banners, on signs, in discussions. After the police raid on the encampment in October, several different people independently conceived that idea. Regardless of who ended up bringing the proposal to the general assembly that afternoon, it was already in the air.

In fact, all the important decisions that were passed in the General Assembly were ideas that already had force. It wasn't that the General Assembly gave them force—they already had it. But there was something about the General Assembly, where you had to go through the motions of bringing a proposal that had already been agreed upon so it could be understood as official. This is where the question of the General Assembly as a legitimate decision-making body comes in.

B: But it wasn't just a matter of legitimizing things—it was also a question of coordinating them. For example, for the general strike, we had ten or fifteen different groups distributing fliers in different parts of the Bay Area.

T: It was also important that there were so many other assemblies. There was the General Assembly, but there were also all these spin-off assemblies . . .

Those were different from the working groups?

T: They were working groups, but all of them were run as assemblies. And some of them got quite large at times.

The blockade of the port of Oakland during the strike.

So you were saying that it was already determined before the General Assembly whether something could happen . . . does that mean that the debates that really determined what would happen did not take place in the General Assembly, but elsewhere?

P: Sometimes. Sometimes they did. But most of it was that everyone was just talking politics the whole time, everywhere you went, in the encampment or on the street or at home. If you weren't eating or smoking weed, you were probably talking politics. I mean, if you were eating or smoking weed, you were talking politics, too.

So we can understand the consensus process of the General Assembly as a sort of formal ceremony in which the participants established that they were already on the same page about something?

T: That is . . . the optimistic way of looking at it. There is a darker side, which is that even if we all agreed on something in the camp and in our day-to-day interactions, it still wouldn't hap-

A march to attempt to occupy a vacant building in Oakland on January 28, 2012.

pen unless we went through this sort of parliamentary process to give it the official stamp of the Occupy General Assembly. That's how I viewed the general strike: even if it was agreed beforehand, even if the decision had already been made by everyone, we still had to go through this formal performance or else it wouldn't happen.

P: Maybe that's why, towards the end of Occupy Oakland, the General Assembly became a formal body that just gave its stamp of approval in a totally meaningless, ineffectual way. People who had not been involved in it would bring these proposals, and literally all they were asking for was a stamp of approval. The structure had become totally disconnected from the social movement.

T: And they thought that if they got the stamp of approval for their actions, that would mean that those actions would be as big as everything else had been, and everyone in Occupy Oakland would have to go to them. But that was not how it worked at all. Things had to happen organically, they couldn't be declared from the top down.

But there was at least one situation later in which the General Assembly intervened and shut down one of the working groups, as if it had jurisdiction over it. I'm talking about when the media group was disbanded.

T: I think that was an important shift. That was the only time that the General Assembly stepped in and disbanded a group that had been operating autonomously. I stood by that, because the media group had put out a statement that was totally racist, based on a report that was proven to be false . . . I mean, I thought they should disband. And when the Assembly voted that they had to, they did.

B: And that is a slippery slope. I agree, it's good that they were disbanded. But that is a dangerous path to start down. Because what happens when autonomous elements emerge that we don't agree with? Do you use the assembly to control the movement?

The conflict with the media working group is interesting to me because basically, we're talking about rival forms of representation here. If you were saying that the General Assembly functioned as a space where participants in Occupy Oakland could represent themselves to each other as sharing commitment to a project, and perhaps that was a necessary means of getting everyone on the same page, we can understand the media as serving a similar function.

In many Occupy groups, there were conflicts about media representation—we used to joke about the provisional dictatorship of the media working group. Those groups had tremendous power because media is also a way of depicting us to ourselves and each other, in order to dictate what we agree on and believe in. Those portrayals shape what we expect from each other and what we consider ourselves to be capable of.

And that's precisely what the democratic process does: it represents us to ourselves.

S: That's what I'm thinking about, listening to you all reflecting on this. The question is basically what gives people the feeling that they can do things? Even if many people didn't consider the General Assembly to be a governing body, despite the phone trees and the efforts to stack the discussions, eventually, as things escalated, it became the center of everything, the unifying space, and we all shared this enormous belief in what it could accomplish on the basis of what we had done together already. But the assembly was just this thing that we were giving our power to, just like every Democrat or American citizen gives their power to institutions. It was just our radicalized version of it.

I think it's possible that we could have built that shared belief in our power on something else, and that could have saved us from some of the problems that happened later on. Deep in our psyches as Americans, we have this image of people gathered in a political assembly, making decisions. It's one of our founding myths. We could recognize the General Assembly as a distorted version of something that was already familiar, something that already had power in our imaginations. And it wasn't just us—all the liberal people who came into the movement after the raid brought those same associations with them, that same mythology, and many of them didn't believe in autonomy or anything like that.

Don't get me wrong, it's amazing what we did, what Occupy Oakland did. The spirit behind it was amazing. But why did that spirit dissipate, really? Maybe because we based it in that representative structure. When the assembly becomes an institution that represents us to ourselves, when it represents what is possible and what we are capable of, it becomes dangerous. All the times that the assembly would put its stamp on something, and then nothing would happen, that chipped away our belief in ourselves as a force, which chipped away at our ability to act, and that became a degenerative feedback loop. The things that worked didn't happen because they were endorsed by the assembly—they worked because we invested everything in them together.

So yes, we should be open to new opportunities, new models, but we should always remember their limitations, and we should remember that their power comes from us. We should never let them make us lose faith in ourselves.

"Gotov je!"

Direct Democracy in the Slovenian Uprising

A cold winter night. Smoke and pepper spray mingle in the air. From behind our backs, we hear the roaring of thousands and thousands of throats: "They [the politicians] are all finished! We will carry them all out!" In front of us, a burning fence, lines of riot police, and—in the foggy distance—the ultimate symbol of democracy, a parliamentary building. On our faces the cold breeze, beside us the shoulders of our comrades, and in our veins—electricity. Several months into the uprising, the streets are still ours. What started as a protest against a few "bad seeds" in the government has opened up a massive opportunity to think beyond what exists. For a brief moment, we have gained control over our lives, we experiment with creating spaces of togetherness beyond hierarchies, we allow ourselves to dream the impossible. In every second, as we discover our weakness, we also dare to regain our strength.

If only we knew then that it would not be (just) state violence, the natural cycle of the movement, or the court dates, but (mostly) democracy, that would drag us back into reality.

In winter 2012-13, a massive wave of protests swept Slovenia, a small country in the northern Balkans. It started in the second largest city, Maribor, a de-industrialized husk that was once the center of Slovenia's vanished automobile industry. The corrupt mayor had installed speed-checking radar at every major crossroads, resulting in hundreds of already impoverished people being charged with penalties they could not afford to pay, for the profit of a private company. In a series of clandestine attacks and public demonstrations, people burned the speed-checking devices one by one, then gathered on the squares and streets to inform the mayor by means of Molotov cocktails, rocks, and everything else they could get hold of that he was no longer welcome in their town. In response to the initial police repression, solidarity protests spread around the country in a matter of a few days. They lasted for six months.

Images of politicians burning in front of the Slovenian parliament during the uprising, January 2013.

On the one hand, these protests were a reaction to the disastrous effects of the transition from socialism to free market capitalism, which left many people poor and humiliated. On the other hand, from the beginning, they were clearly aimed against those who held institutional political power. This was the biggest self-organized struggle in Slovenia since the breakup of Yugoslavia in 1991. It brought down the mayor of Maribor and the national government—but more importantly, it opened up a space in which it became possible to invent new forms of autonomous action and to question representative democracy.

Although the effects of this period cannot be reduced to the fact of defeat, it is interesting to note how rapidly much of the radical energy was channeled back into the existing order, and the central role that the language of democracy played in this. The fall of the government and the promise of a new election was the first nail in the coffin of the struggle, as it satisfied a lot of people who then began to withdraw from the streets. Meanwhile, a new political party on the left did its best to

"Gotov je!" ["He is finished!"]

– A slogan from the uprising of 2012-2013, directed at the representatives of democratic order.

monopolize speaking for the uprising; eventually, it emerged as a shining star in the new political order by promising more direct democracy in the parliament—the same parliament that had been the object of so much rage and disillusionment only weeks earlier. Finally, in Maribor, where the rebellion started, the next mayor who was elected came from the ranks of the uprising, from a civil society group. He promised to revitalize democracy in Maribor and to carry out economic development, but the people who elected him were swiftly disappointed. By 2015, he was being investigated for corruption, with the City Council calling for his resignation.

So . . . has direct democracy contributed to the continued radicalization of Slovenian society?

The uprising was just one stage in a long line of struggles in Slovenia that continue to this day—from the squatting movement in the early 1990s and 2000s, through the anti-war and anti-NATO campaigns, to student occupations, self-organized wildcat strikes, anti-fascist struggles, and most recently, the opening of Fortress Europe to migration along the Balkan route. Throughout these struggles, many anarchists and other radicals believed that spreading directly democratic methods was one of the key elements that we could contribute to radicalize movements and keep them beyond the control of representative democracy, hierarchical structures, and reformist politics. It took years to realize that investing our energy in making assemblies the organizational crux of those movements might have been a step away from what we wanted to achieve. Today, some of

Protesters tearing down the fence in front of the Slovenian parliament, January 2013.

us are beginning to think about how we might shift from the concept of direct democracy towards another framework.

This doesn't mean rejecting the assembly as an organizational model. The assemblies often helped to bring people onto the streets and into the struggle; they were an important tool for organizing. However, the long-term results were often disappointing. It was easy to blame the way assemblies were organized and our lack of energy for participating in them on the various hostile forces determined to prevent these movements from spreading throughout society. But after we had mastered the game of consensus, the art of facilitation, and all the accompanying hand signals, some of us began to question the concept of direct democracy itself. Maybe we could approach those assemblies as opportunities for some other kind of togetherness—not as a space of government, but sites via which to disperse power into our communities.

We have no universal truths to offer. These are simply the reflections of a few people on a few years of struggle. Here is what we think we have learned so far.

Occupations and the Democracy of Direct Action

"I am a part of this because I think direct democracy is better than the order we know now. With direct democracy, if you want something, you say it, find friends to help you, and you do it."

In 2011, new occupation movements were seizing squares all over the world. In Spain, people came out to the streets in the movement later known as 15M; in the US, it was known as Occupy. In Slovenia, as in many other parts of Europe, the first occupation started out as a protest against financial capitalism on October 15, 2011. Consequently, in Ljubljana, the movement came to be known as 15O. The occupation of the square in front of the stock exchange lasted six months.

This occupation brought out into the open all the divisions in society that are otherwise hidden. Poverty, drug addiction, homelessness, mental health problems, the misery of everyday life under capitalism—all of these became visible to everyone, so they could no longer be dismissed as a matter of personal failure. The 15O movement did not center only on the demand for real democracy; rather, it attacked financialization, capitalism, precarity, austerity, total institutions, and representational politics. No topic was too small; for many, the camp and the assemblies became platforms to discuss if not organize for every political activity in the city. Particularly in the first weeks of the occupation, the camp was just one of many playful direct actions taking place all around the city.

Tired of being talked at about what ought to be done by people who didn't take initiative themselves, participants in the movement developed the concept of "democracy of direct action" (DDA). This basically meant that if you proposed something, you should also participate in it. In that sense, the values of DDA helped to foster autonomous action rather than centralizing

The occupation in front of the Stock Exchange at the beginning of
the 15O movement in October 2011. Borza, "Stock Exchange," has
been changed to Bojza, "struggle for."

democratic decision-making processes in the assembly. As a
result, the culture that developed in the movement was oriented
towards action, mostly in the form of efforts to communicate
with the general public through various kinds of performance.

DDA had disadvantages as well. As often happens in a
variety of structures, it (unreflectively) favored those who were
articulate enough to attract more people to their initiatives.
The multiplicity of actions carried out by a relatively small
number of participants in the movement also meant that energy
was widely dispersed, efforts were often not interlinked, and
overextended comrades often struggled with burnout. Along
with the distribution of political projects among a variety of
working groups, DDA helped to create several different sites of
decision-making; yet it did not generate a space of encounter
in which people came together for mutual learning to create
a meaningful force beyond direct democracy.

The daily assemblies became focused on camp issues, and
there were fewer and fewer participants, while the monthly

assemblies focused more on the political content of the movement. Those who were involved in the working groups but not sleeping in the camp eventually felt alienated by it. In the end, 15O ended in exhaustion and frustration. Many were driven into isolation and depression.

However, 15O taught us several important lessons. First, despite all the talk about direct democracy as a positive aspect of the Occupy movements, some participants in 15O concluded from firsthand experience that the concentration of legitimacy in a single site of decision-making was not productive. Did it make sense to understand what was happening in the occupation in front of the stock exchange as a directly democratic movement, when all the groundbreaking and exciting things developed outside of consensus-based democratic procedures? Perhaps if we had made the question of how to promote decentralized action central to our thinking, we could have avoided all the problems that resulted from centralizing the assembly. If we hadn't informally institutionalized the assemblies, taking them for granted as the foundation of the movement, maybe we would have been able recognize the moments when we had the potential to make a big impact, and, later, to realize that we had been successfully marginalized. Perhaps we would have been more capable of asking ourselves which tactics were advancing our agendas, and which ones were just draining us when it was time to move on.

The Limitations of Assemblies in the Student Movement

"If they don't meet our demands, we can always be more radical and occupy more space in the university later. For now, let's just show our strength."

Ljubljana, November 2011. On one side of town, tents have occupied the square in front of the stock exchange for a month and a half. On the other side of town, students are packed into one of the biggest lecture rooms in the Faculty of Arts. The assembly has only one item on the agenda: whether to occupy the faculty to prevent the privatization of higher education.

Some of us arrived ready to block the production of knowledge in the entire building, in hopes that such a radical act would open up the space and shake up the power relations in the university. We thought it would be better for the movement to be evicted after three days, still ready to keep fighting, than to exhaust itself in a limited occupation that did not disrupt the status quo of the university, let alone society at large. Others assumed that it would be enough to occupy a few classrooms and open negotiations with the authorities. After hours of discussion, a few professors and student leaders persuaded the majority of people to vote against a full blockade.

For those of us who were left in the minority—whether or not we wanted to vote in first place—the choice was tough. We thought about whether to go against the decision of the assembly and occupy the entire building on our own, at the risk of alienating ourselves from the others. In the end, we went along with the decision of the assembly. Looking back, we should probably have acted differently.

The partial occupation lasted for a few months. At first, the university administration was still trying to negotiate, not knowing how far the protests might go. But they soon realized they did not need to comply with any of the demands. The occupiers even gave up some of the classrooms themselves, feeling that they were not capable of filling them with their own self-organized study projects. Instead of the end of the occupation opening a wider conflict in society or drawing more people into the struggle, it left the student movement exhausted and scattered, limited to negotiating with the school authorities through the existing system of representation. There has not been an occupation in any university in Slovenia since.

And anarchists? We tried to participate in a self-organized study process, but mostly it felt like we were talking to ourselves.

The meeting at the beginning of the occupation of the Faculty of Arts in Ljubljana in November 2011.

It took months of frustration to realize that in accepting the norms of democratic decision-making, we had failed to push the moment further, missing the chance to open up productive conflicts—within the movement, inside the university, and in society as a whole. At the least, we could have started a much-needed discussion about which tactics the movement should be using, and how to decide which tactics were legitimate. But instead of setting our own agenda, we had accepted others' priorities and lost ourselves in the process. The problem was not the assembly itself, but rather that this body was understood as the only place of decision-making, so no action outside of it seemed legitimate—even to us.

Building Institutions or Opening up Space?

"By organizing assemblies, we wish to open new spaces of articulation of common power, that will be growing as we exchange experiences, knowledge, and opinions in order to build a common space of equality, freedom, and solidarity."

– Invitation to the first "Open Uprising Assembly" in Ljubljana, late December 2012.

A few months after the end of 15O, the uprising started. But no one hurried to convene assemblies. The first few weeks of activity in Ljubljana saw a variety of decentralized actions, protests, discussions, and meetings. When it became clear that certain organized groups within the uprising were trying to determine and represent the movement's demands in order to steer the movement in a centralized and predictable direction, other participants introduced assemblies as a tool to prevent centralization and unification, rather than as a method for being "directly democratic." By gathering many different participants into one place, the assembly created an infrastructure in which every attempt to establish hierarchies would be visible to everyone and therefore questioned and rejected.

From the beginning, the "Uprising Open Assembly" was positioned as only one of several different ways of coordinating, communicating, and building common power. The aim was to create a space of convergence and encounter, but never to let it become the sole decision-making space for the uprising as a whole. This was a place for people who wanted to do similar things to find each other, and to discuss problematic occurrences—for instance, it was the platform in which people attacked nationalism.

One of the biggest achievements of those assemblies was that they served to communicate radical approaches to people who were not yet using them. The value of a diversity of tactics gained recognition in the assemblies; as a result of the discussions, many participants committed themselves to solidarity with all forms of protest. During the first few protests, some people had actively turned over demonstrators dressed in black to the police; towards the end of the uprising, when a few protesters were arrested, hundreds of people ran to the police station and blocked it until they were released.

Although the uprising maintained its intensity for half a year, only a few assemblies took place in Ljubljana during that period. Based on our negative experiences in the two preceding movements, we felt that if the assembly was to be a tool for the movement rather than an end in itself, it was important to know when to drop it. When fewer people were showing up on the streets, it became obvious that we needed to move on, not to try to recreate a situation that had already passed. At the point when the assemblies could have become just a space of nostalgic behavior, we refused to call for another; instead, we started thinking about where a new point of conflict might emerge, and how to organize around it.

Maribor had a different experience. Neighborhood assemblies covering roughly half of the city were still happening there in 2016, over three years after the end of uprising. These mostly focused on self-organizing daily life in various neighborhoods. Some speculate that the assemblies continued in Maribor but not in Ljubljana because there was a greater need for practical self-organization in a city laid waste by de-industrialization. Others have argued that the assemblies have continued in Maribor because one of the groups there made it a priority to maintain them as their primary project. The open question here is whether such assemblies can produce radical content—or is it enough that they are using a supposedly radical form? What if the people participating in the neighborhood assemblies use them to pursue reactionary goals? Does it make sense to promote radical values along with the tactic of assembly? Is it enough to open up that space?

In the uprising, despite going against and beyond the concepts of direct democracy in our practices, we were still using that term to describe many of our actions. This became

The uprising in Maribor, December 3, 2012.

a problem—not so much in the assemblies themselves, but in connection with other outcomes of the uprising. While it seemed that anarchists and anti-authoritarian ideas were at the forefront of the diverse actions on the ground, the representation of the uprising to the public fell to people who later formed a political party along the lines of Syriza, promising more direct democracy in the parliament and a productive relationship with social movements. Would they have been able to pull this off if we had not helped promote the language of direct democracy?

Against and Beyond (Direct) Democracy

When the uprising was dying, people wondered how to transmit the connections we'd built in the streets into our everyday lives. In one of the assemblies in Ljubljana, people formed a working group to organize in the neighborhoods, hoping to radicalize

March in Ljubljana during the uprising, December 2012.

people there by setting up a structure in which people could
self-organize.

We never wanted to be the professional organizers of the
resistance, so we only organized in the neighborhoods where
we lived; likewise, we intended to rotate roles as much as possible. During the peak of the uprising, when the frequency of
actions was so overwhelming that it was hard to keep track
of them all, it had been easy enough to utilize the assembly
as a tool without it becoming an end in itself. This grew more
difficult when there was no one left on the streets and the assemblies became the only form of action in the neighborhoods.
Despite good turnouts at the neighborhood assemblies, we
soon realized that people were relying on us to organize and
facilitate the meetings. All of the working groups wanted us to
be involved, to such an extent that we felt that it was no longer
a self-organized process. We realized that it was better not to
have assemblies at all than to have them organized by a few.
We didn't want to accept a position of authority in this way.

For the city government, however, this was not an obstacle.
When we heard that a neighborhood where we were not
organizing had also started to hold assemblies, at first we
thought that we were finally seeing authentic self-organization.

Unfortunately, it turned out to be an intervention orchestrated by the city government through a Non-Governmental Organization (NGO). They were financing people to work on the project of "self-organization." The city government had coopted the framework of direct democracy, using it as a tool to neutralize any potential for dissent that might emerge from that neighborhood.

When the state is sponsoring direct democracy, we have to ask ourselves how we could prevent this kind of cooptation. Is it a good idea to make movements depend on a tool that is so easily turned against them? What if the problem is not that our assemblies need to be improved, but that there is nothing inherent in direct democracy that differentiates it from the state? When people began to succeed in overthrowing monarchies, the state persisted through the introduction of representative democracy. All its institutions and functions remain intact, with the sole difference that now they are administered by elected representatives rather than hereditary sovereigns. Could direct democracy be a new version of this compromise, once again preserving the uneven distribution of power while giving us the illusion of self-determination?

And in this situation, when we still need to create opportunities to engage in open discussion and realize our full potential through our intersections with one another—will the assembly continue to play a part in this process? Probably. But we may have to approach it differently, not as a tool of direct democracy but rather as a platform for connecting and coordinating autonomous actions and groups. In 2016, we saw an example of this in the Anti-Racist Front, a space for individuals and groups active in migrant struggles.

This is our conclusion coming out of several years of experimentation with direct democracy in Slovenia: we are tentatively retaining the forms, but we need to ditch the discourse.

Born in Flames, Died in Plenums

The Bosnian Experiment with Direct Democracy, 2014

"The war is still going on."

– Graffiti in Mostar

In February 2014, two decades after the war that left Bosnia devastated and divided into three ethnic regions, the country erupted in flames again. This time, it was not ethnic strife, but the rage of people uniting against politicians. For years, these politicians had stirred up ethnic divisions to distract the people while systematically looting the country. The result was intense poverty: unemployment was at 44 percent in 2014, and up to 60 percent among the young.

People flooded into the streets. Beating back the police, they burned the parliament and municipal buildings. In the turmoil of the protests, panicking politicians stole money from the national treasury and prepared to flee the country. In Mostar, a city divided between Muslims and Catholics, several politicians sent their families into Croatia through the nearby border. Protests under the slogans "Freedom is my nation" and "Let's fire all the politicians" drew crowds in 33 cities. People gathered to experiment with direct democracy in assemblies (dubbed plenums) of up to a thousand—something that had not been seen on such a scale in any ex-Yugoslavian country since the last Balkan wars.* Outside Bosnia, partisans of direct democracy expressed considerable enthusiasm about what some called the Bosnian Spring.

---

* The 2014 uprising didn't appear out of thin air. In 2006, a movement called Dosta (Enough) grew from a small internet forum into weekly meetings in the central square in Sarajevo, getting bigger every week and addressing economic and social issues through discussions that eventually gave rise to protests. As the organizational structure of Dosta spread into different cities, it remained politically diverse. Several of the most active participants in the plenums in Sarajevo had been radicalized in the Dosta movement.

Angry and disillusioned in Bosnia.

There were many inspiring things about the 2014 uprising—the rejection of nationalism and representative democracy, the visibility of women protesting in a largely patriarchal society, the focus on social and economic struggles rather than ethnic hatred. Many people from all sectors of society were radicalized through the protests.

However, the uprising abated just as the plenums were getting off the ground. At the time, many saw the plenums as the next step after the riots: once the police had been defeated and the politicians put on the defensive, it was time for people to get together and figure out what they wanted instead. Yet a few months later, the government had reasserted control, the plenums had lost all their leverage, and it was back to business as usual.

What defeated the uprising? Was it repression in the streets, or pacification in the plenums? Was it the division between riot and plenum? Or would it have died anyway?

February 7, 2014: Protesters burning documents in front of a burning government building in Tuzla. The graffiti reads "death to nationalism" and "all politicians must go."

"Where were you when we were fighting on the streets?" the old worker demanded of the young people who had facilitated the plenums six months prior. He was still protesting in front of the parliament in Sarajevo every day—only now, he and his friends were on their own, just like they had been before the uprising.

The Plenum vs. the Street

At the beginning, the plenums were an organic expression of the struggle on the streets. Like the protests, they drew people who had never participated in such struggles before. Some people did not feel comfortable in the clashes, yet wanted to speak out about their anger or to articulate their desires for the future. They came together with demonstrators to form directly democratic assemblies: the plenums.

The plenums served many as a kind of collective therapy. They offered a common space in which people could be heard:

for the first time in their lives, they felt that their opinions mattered. They spoke about the war, about post-traumatic stress, about their living conditions, about their hatred of the system that had humiliated them to such an extent that they no longer felt like human beings. "Struggle gave us our dignity back," many people said.

The procedures of the plenums were intended to keep power horizontal: roles rotated between participants, speakers were limited to a few minutes each, the facilitation was intended to foster inclusiveness and egalitarianism. In some cases, this served to keep the plenums a diverse space. Elsewhere, those who had more formal education were more comfortable in the discussions, as they were used to articulating themselves in a certain public discourse; in some of the plenums, influence accrued in the hands of intellectuals like Asim Mujkić, a professor of political science who repeatedly represented the Sarajevo plenum in the media. Meanwhile, some people who had participated in the demonstrations did not come to the plenums; others came at first, then stopped coming. Some apparently trusted the plenums to represent their needs, whether they attended or not. Others likely resented the idea that anyone was speaking in their name.

Just as attendance at the plenums was dying down, the police were quietly reestablishing control of the streets. The city governments set back up in smaller offices outside the burned buildings.

"What about the people who burned the buildings?" I asked. "Did they participate in the plenums here in Tuzla?"

"No," she answered, "They didn't. They sent a representative to the first plenum, before things really got going. He said that if the government didn't change its tune, they were going to burn the buildings. But after that, none of them came to the plenums."

I could understand why people who had just burnt down the headquarters of the government would be hesitant to show up to public meetings. Indeed, not long after everything died down, the police began doling out terrorism charges. At the

February, 2014: The authorities lose control.

same time, what kind of sense does it make to burn down the offices of the government, and then present petitions to them? It seemed to me that the revolt was doomed from the moment that a separation emerged between fighting the old order and creating a new one.

Institutions vs. Tools

The plenum facilitators and the most active organizers of working groups, who had initiated their efforts in an honest attempt to spread the struggle into other spheres of life, found themselves in a position of de facto authority. They were the ones setting the agenda and determining the course of discussions; they became the names and faces of the uprising. It was up to them, it seemed, to identify, express, and prioritize the demands that had driven people to rise up. Most of these organizers never wanted that kind of power—but they wanted the uprising to succeed in changing Bosnian society, and they believed that the plenums were essential to this.

February 14, 2014: A plenum in Sarajevo demands the establishment of a "nonparty expert government."

Most of the facilitators were committed to the principles of direct democracy. They believed that adhering to directly democratic procedures in the assemblies would stave off power imbalances and bureaucracy. But already, in this hope, a subtle shift had taken place: rather than vesting legitimacy in the needs and desires of the participants in the uprising, they were beginning to vest it in the plenums as institutions. Instead of serving as one tool among many with which to solve problems and meet needs, the plenums were becoming an end unto themselves.

As the demonstrations came to an end, the plenums ceased serving as a tool to reinforce the actions people took in the streets. More and more, they took on the role of a traditional protest organization, a sort of watchdog monitoring the government. Only without teeth.

"We didn't mean to end up in that situation," said one of the former facilitators of the Sarajevo plenums. "We wanted to help, but not to have so much control over the process. It wasn't clear to us at the time that it was happening that way."

Presenting Demands vs. Building a Common Language of Struggle

The riots of spring 2014 gave Bosnian politicians a scare for the first time in many years. As soon as they felt safe again, they retaliated on several fronts. Hoping to discredit protesters in the media, they compared burning the parliament in Sarajevo to Serbian aggression during the siege; this set the stage for them to press terrorism charges later. At the same time, they attempted to channel the movement back into conventional politics, making it less radical, less unpredictable, less uncontrollable. Unfortunately, the plenums turned out to be conducive to this effort.

The Bosnian uprising gave voice to thousands of individual desires, ideas, and needs. But rather than connecting these in a common language of struggle that could preserve what was unique in each while creating a platform for people to act in concert, the consensus-building process of the plenums served to reduce this diversity of voices to a few basic demands.

In an attempt to strengthen the leverage of the plenums, the plenums of various cities made contact and undertook to formulate a list of common demands. Working groups that consisted of fewer and fewer people worked through thousands of demands, joining some together, interpreting and adjusting others, discarding some altogether. It took them until April 9, two months after the riots, to present the common demands of all the plenums to the government at a symbolic protest in Sarajevo.

They received no response. By the time the plenums had reduced everyone's rage to a few demands, the government did not need to care anymore. This was the last nail in the coffin of the uprising.

"When you came here from Slovenia and told us that the movement would die in the assemblies," he said, "I didn't believe you. But it happened just the way you said it would."

February 21, 2014: Participants in the Sarajevo plenum listen to spokespeople from the Fojnica, Konjic, and Mostar plenums.

March, 2014: The plenum continues meeting in Sarajevo.

Government vs. Self-Organization

In Tuzla, where the uprising started, the riots had forced the prime minister of the canton to resign. The plenum then demanded that a non-affiliated provisional government be formed until the regular elections. They expected this government to report to the plenum every week. Indeed, they got a provisional government with a professor for prime minister, accompanied by a few ministers who had not been much involved in politics before. Yet it soon turned out that not only were many of these new politicians connected to the established political parties, they were also involved in corruption, which had been one of the immediate causes of the uprising in the first place. It didn't take long for the newly elected politicians to stop communicating with the plenum and its committees. There were new faces in the government, but the elite had preserved its power.

The second-to-last entry on plenumsa.org, the website of the Sarajevo plenum, is about responding to the floods that ravaged Bosnia in May 2014.* Self-organized relief efforts by the participants of plenums were essential to helping many people to weather this disaster, while the government did precious little to help. Yet after that, these sites of self-organization were abandoned. The following October, the elections brought one of the conservative parties back to power in Tuzla—the party rumored to have been pulling the strings of the provisional government all along.

And the leader of this new government? A former minister of the interior, who had been in charge of the police.

"I have one enemy. You are not my enemy, the government is my enemy," the old man shouted, addressing his old comrades from the plenums. "We said everything we had to say to the enemy when we burned the parliament."

* The very last post on plenumsa.org (June 12, 2014) is an interview with a US-based academic about Occupy and direct democracy.

The floods that ravaged Bosnia in May 2014.

Democracy vs. Freedom

Over the past few years, there have been several movements in Bosnia, each of them going a bit further than the last. Each of these movements has brought new people into the streets and then subsided—but the question is what happens next. Do these people continue to develop their capacity to act autonomously, building strength from uprising to uprising? Or do they end up joining the ranks of the political parties?

Basing social struggles on the demand for more democracy—whether representative or direct—is especially seductive in Bosnia, where people feel that the Dayton Agreement that concluded the war in 1995 paralyzed the country by enforcing divisions along ethnic lines throughout the administration and daily life. Many people in Bosnia think that the solution to all their problems would be to create a functional, unified state no longer divided according to the Dayton treaty, incorporating everyone from the three "nations" as fellow citizens. They look approvingly to the countries of northern and western Europe as a model for their own. Even many who consider themselves radicals understand direct democracy as a means to this end, rather than a way of restructuring society from the ground up. This may explain why it was such a short step from the direct democracy of the plenums back to the (barely) representative democracy of the government. When we legitimize our struggles by means of the rhetoric of democracy, it opens the door for the partisans of the status quo to justify the return to normal on the same grounds. Order must be restored so there can be proper elections!

In fact, the same unemployment, poverty, and ethnic strife that have inflicted so much suffering in Bosnia are spreading all around Europe, from Greece to Finland. Modernizing the government and purging it of "corruption" is not enough to turn a country into a wealthy social democracy; in a profit-driven economy, there will never be enough wealth to go around. If we limit ourselves to attempting to reform governments—even if that means replacing them with networks of plenums intended to fulfill the same functions—we will never get to the root of the problem. What would it mean to look at the uprising and the plenums as steps towards a totally different social order, rather than a means to revitalize this one?

Perhaps if the plenums had served as spaces for coordinating ongoing action, they could have propelled the uprising further, organizing new attacks to keep the authorities at bay and generating new forms of life outside the capitalist economy. Once the discussions in the plenums became abstract, it was inevitable that regardless of the participants' and facilitators' intentions they would be reduced to delegating, to representing, to petitioning. As "direct" as the plenums aspired to be, they ended up treating the uprising as an expression of desires that had to be represented, not as a space where those desires could be fulfilled. Once the participants understood the uprising that way, it was only natural to address those desires to the government—the proper representational body—in the form of demands. Those demands could only strengthen the government, fatally weakening the plenums.

The Bosnian uprising of 2014 is just one example out of a long line of experiments with assemblies as a tool of revolt. It appears that the assembly cannot serve as a place for envisioning the

Graffiti in Bosnia.

future and then looking around for some other political body to institute it. That political body will always be the state, which has no need of the assembly except as a means of legitimizing itself. Likewise, the assembly must not become an institution with its own procedures that are regarded as legitimate in and of themselves—if it does, then at best, it will become the state. To play a part in liberation, the assembly has to be a tool via which power is exercised directly according to a different logic, a logic that does not concentrate it but disperses it, promoting the autonomy and freedom of the participants.

"This had to happen," emphasized a young mother in a black hijab, her voice trembling with emotion, as she gestured at the burnt-out shell of the government headquarters in Tuzla. "The buildings had to burn. The uprising was the best thing that ever happened in my life. I hope it will happen again. It has to."

[opposite] Don't turn back: the burnt government building in Tuzla after the uprising.

The Democracy of the Reaction

What the revolutions of 1848 tell us about the limits of 2011

What harm could possibly come of using the discourse of democracy to describe the object of our movements for liberation? We can answer this question with a fable drawn from history: the story of the uprising that took place in Paris in June 1848.

In The Democracy Project, David Graeber draws parallels between the revolutions of 1848 and the uprisings of 2011. None of the revolutionary movements of 1848 managed to hold power for more than a couple years, he notes, yet the basic goals that they fought for were widely achieved within a few decades: everywhere, monarchies were giving way to constitutional democracies, with universal suffrage and social safety nets on the way. The argument by analogy is that, though the uprisings that peaked in 2011 were not immediately successful, they will have a long-term impact on how we think about politics. The struggles for state democracy in the Middle East and Southeast Asia and the experiences of directly democratic movements in Europe and the US created a situation in which people around the world are bound to demand more democracy in their governments and their lives.

Perhaps. But this framework doesn't offer us any tools with which to understand how the reactionary forces that suffered

> "What is wonderful about universal suffrage is that it nips riot in the bud and, by giving the vote to insurrection, disarms it."

> – Victor Hugo, *Les Misérables*

setbacks in 1848 and 2011 could reconfigure themselves under democratic banners. In Egypt, after the revolution of 2011, the idea of democratic government re-legitimized the apparatus of state repression long enough for the military to regain its stranglehold on power. In Europe and the US, the momentum of directly democratic grassroots movements was channeled into political parties like Syriza and Podemos and the doomed candidacy of Bernie Sanders—none of which were able to deliver on their promises.

In fact, what happened in Egypt between 2011 and 2014 is a lot like what happened in France between 1848 and 1851. A wide-ranging coalition of different groups overthrew a dictator; the most conservative elements in the coalition won the elections; the resulting popular uprisings were repressed in the name of protecting the fledgling democracy; and in the end, a new despot came to power on a law-and-order platform through a combination of election and coup.

The reemergence of the Deep State* in France by June 1848 and in Egypt between 2011 and 2013 underscores why ever since 1848 anarchists have argued that the only sure way to hold on to revolutionary gains is to delegitimize and disarticulate the state itself. In this regard, the problem with democratic discourse is that, because the vast majority of democratic models are state-based, it offers cover to anyone who wants to re-legitimize state

---

* The Deep State is the institutional elements of the state that persist from one elected government to the next, such as the military and intelligence apparatus, and the interests that they serve.

power. Indeed, even those who explicitly oppose the state can end up reinforcing it—whether by joining the government, as anarchists from the CNT did during the Spanish Civil War, or more obliquely, by legitimizing frameworks and objectives that ultimately enable partisans of the state to present themselves as the ones with the most effective strategy, as anarchists like Cindy Milstein and David Graeber risk doing.

To understand how this works, let's go back to 1848.

In February 1848, an uprising in Paris toppled the king; revolt radiated throughout Europe along with the news of the French revolution, spreading faster than any wave of unrest in the digital age. The transformation of France into a Republic occasioned much rejoicing, but there was little agreement as to what a Republic was. Just as anarchists, socialists, liberals, neoconservatives, and fascists rub shoulders under the banner of democracy today, in 1848 a vast range of people identified with the ideal of the Republic, confining themselves to debates about what the true nature of the Republic might be. Even Pierre-Joseph Proudhon, already a self-professed anarchist, called himself a Republican,† and his explicit opposition to authority didn't stop him from serving in the National Assembly alongside conservatives like Adolphe Thiers—the statesman who later butchered the Paris Commune to baptize the conservative Third Republic.

Indeed, universal manhood suffrage, long sought by radicals, brought a predominantly reactionary government to power. Former monarchists and aristocrats reinvented themselves as Republicans and set out to use their superior resources to game the system. All this illustrates why, once a goal is achieved, it's best to dispense with the old rhetoric in favor of language that

† Notably, in his first significant work, *What Is Property*, in the same passage in which he first identifies himself as an anarchist. Despite his uneven track record, Proudhon's critical reflections on democracy, published at the outset of the 1848 revolution in *The Solution of the Social Problem*, diagnose many of the contradictions that today's partisans of democracy have yet to recognize.

The barricades of June 1848.

clarifies the new problems that arise. Today, we can't imagine anarchists or other sincere proponents of freedom laying claim to the banner of the Republic, though many still present themselves as the champions of real democracy.

In June 1848, four months after the revolution, the newly elected government of the Republic rescinded the few steps it had taken to address the plight of the poor—and the workers who had risen up in February once again barricaded the streets of Paris and called for revolution. From the perspective of the good Republicans, this was unthinkable: they had finally achieved a democratic government, so anyone who revolted against it was an enemy of democracy. This time, the workers found no allies among middle-class Republicans. They were on their own.

Victor Hugo, elected to the National Assembly alongside Proudhon and Thiers, considered it his civic duty as a democrat and Republican to accompany the army as it stormed the city and gunned down the rebels. The reactionaries who had not been able to vanquish the workers in the name of the monarchy now slaughtered them in the name of the Republic, preserving the social order that had caused the revolution in the first place. Thousands were massacred in a three-day hail of lead. Afterward, many shops could not reopen because all the employees had been killed.

A few months later, Napoleon's nephew was elected President of the Republic, promising to reassert order in France. At the end of his term, he organized a coup d'etat to establish himself as Emperor, bringing the brief reign of democracy to an end. This time, Victor Hugo implored the workers of Paris to build barricades and rise against the usurper. Not surprisingly, they turned the poet a deaf ear.* Why should they risk their lives to preserve the authority of the Republicans who had massacred them last time they rose against their oppressors?

Now that the Reaction had no more use for the politicians who had paved the way for it, they too were herded into prison and exile. Hugo escaped to the island of Guernsey; some of his fellow representatives were killed outright. Their elections and patriotism had served to maintain the legitimacy of the government just long enough for a shrewder tyrant to take the helm. Urging the poor to break the law in the name of the Constitution, Victor Hugo and his comrades showed the contradictions inherent in their lukewarm revolutionism. They paid a steep price for their naïveté—mostly with others' blood.

With the novels he published from exile, Hugo earned worldwide acclaim for putting words in the mouths of the same poor people whose slaughter he had overseen. He wrote about the events of June 1848 in his memoirs, bewailing "on one side the despair of the people, on the other the despair of society," sidestepping his role in the killings he described with such pathos. In Les Misérables, he struggled to make sense of how the people who had made the revolution could take up arms against its legitimately elected representatives:

* You can read Victor Hugo's blow-by-blow account of these events in his *Histoire d'un crime*.

It sometimes happens that, even contrary to principles, even contrary to liberty, equality, and fraternity, even contrary to the universal vote, even contrary to the government, by all for all, from the depths of its anguish, of its discouragements and its destitutions, of its fevers, of its distresses, of its miasmas, of its ignorances, of its darkness, that great and despairing body, the rabble, protests against, and that the populace wages battle against, the people.

It was necessary to combat it, and this was a duty, for it attacked the republic. But what was June, 1848, at bottom? A revolt of the people against itself . . . It attacked in the name of the revolution—what? The revolution. It—that barricade, chance, hazard, disorder, terror, misunderstanding, the unknown—faced the Constituent Assembly, the sovereignty of the people, universal suffrage, the nation, the Republic.

Victor Hugo sided with society against the people who comprise it; with sovereignty against liberty; with humanity against human beings. In the name of democracy and the republic, he hoodwinked himself into doing his part to preserve class society at the barrel of a gun. He wasn't alone in this: Proudhon and practically all the well-known socialists kept to the government's side of the barricades.

At the time, republican democracy was new enough to Europe that few could foresee how it might advance a reactionary agenda. The same is true of direct democracy today: it has occurred to very few people that a more participatory digital democracy could actually buttress the legitimacy of police and prisons. Graeber's prediction—that the democratic aims of the movements defeated in 2011 will nonetheless be achieved in the years ahead—might be fulfilled without achieving any significant gains towards liberation, just as the agendas of the revolutions of 1848 were implemented in a repressive way by politicians like Adolphe Thiers who killed off the original revolutionaries in the process. The French Republic finally triumphed in 1871 with the massacre of tens of thousands of Communards; just like the workers of June 1848, the generations of anarchists and communists that came after 1871 had to fight against the republican government without the assistance of those who had joined them in opposing the monarchy and the emperor. Contrary to Graeber's optimism, the aspirations of 1848 were realized in letter but not in spirit—as too might the aspirations of 2011 be, unless we develop a critique of the democracy of the reaction.

How can we avoid repeating the tragedy of June 1848? First, we should never let a shift in the political sphere substitute for social and economic self-determination. Likewise, we should never become so enamored of a particular decision-making method—be it parliamentary democracy or consensus-run assemblies—that we can be induced to countenance injustice in its name. In every Occupy camp in which middle-class participants used the general assembly to lord it over homeless occupants of the encampment, we can recognize an echo of June 1848.

Finally, above all, we should always be thinking beyond our own victories, developing critical tools with which to tackle the problems that will arise afterwards—fighting the next war, not the last one.

Conclusion:
Secessio Plebis

In ancient Rome, when the common people wanted to force the nobility to grant them more political rights, the whole plebian class would climb a hill and refused to come down until their demands were granted. This was called secessio plebis: secession of the people.

The world was smaller then and things were simpler. Today, automation and neoliberal globalization are diminishing the ways that the rich and powerful depend on the rest of the population. This explains why the strike offers us less and less leverage on those who hold power.

In this situation, it is less realistic to seek equal status in the reigning order than to break with it once and for all. The future is not inclusion—it is autonomy. Rather than going out on strike, we must strike out on our own.

Yet the political model Rome developed has colonized the whole world. When in Rome, we're told, do as the Romans do—but Rome's boundaries have expanded so far that there is no hill left to climb. We have to secede right here, in the heart of the empire: not to present demands to our rulers, but to seize back the resources they have taken from us, creating spaces beyond their control in which power flows according to a different logic.

It's a tall order. But if we can open a rift in the fabric of empire, surely countless others will pour through it alongside us.

As we were completing this book, history seemed to be racing ahead of us. The UK voted in a referendum to leave the European Union—the autocratic Turkish government thwarted a coup in which both sides claimed to be defending democracy—a reactionary populist movement brought about the impeachment of Brazilian President Dilma Rousseff—and finally, Donald Trump became President of the United States. In all of these cases, democratic rhetoric and practices legitimized the consolidation of repressive regimes and xenophobic nationalism. All of them came as a shock to those who assume that democracy goes hand in hand with progressive politics.

On the contrary, we are entering an era in which the discourse of democracy will be used to advance more and more reactionary agendas. This should come as no surprise from the mode of government under which Adolf Hitler came to power. In a globalized world, democracy is the operating system of the gated community, promising equality and self-determination while legitimizing repression and xenophobia.

It is more pressing than ever to update the vocabulary with which we describe what we oppose in the prevailing order and what kind of world we want to live in. We humbly put this book at your disposal as one tool in that struggle.

"As we travelled towards a land of liberty, my heart would at times leap for joy. At other times, being, as I was, almost constantly on my feet, I felt as though I could travel no further. But when I thought of slavery, with its democratic whips—its republican chains—its evangelical blood-hounds, and its religious slave-holders—when I thought of all this paraphernalia of American democracy and religion behind me, and the prospect of liberty before me, I was encouraged to press forward, my heart was strengthened, and I forgot that I was tired or hungry."

– Narrative of William W. Brown, an American slave, written by himself, 1850

Appendix

THE ART OF POLITICS

A primer for community self-defense

Politics is the art of

Purportedly, it is at once separate from every other sphere of activity and yet qualified to govern all of them. Politics begins where daily experience, individual tastes, passion and poetry and camaraderie leave off—in short, in the absence of everything that can inform people as to how to make decisions in their best interest. Nothing that truly matters—neither the waitress's ennui nor the bureaucrat's insomnia—can be addressed in the political arena, though decisions made in that arena have repercussions everywhere else.

Politics is the art of

There is a proper time, place, and person for every decision; this renders all other times, places, and people improper. From this initial, fundamental exclusion, a host of other exclusions follow. Because politics must remain separate from actual human life, from everything that could give it teeth and a heartbeat, the role of professionals is indisputable—the most that can be done is to replace them from time to time. These professionals may be elected officials, or they may be "community organizers" or even "facilitators." Regardless, the systems they administer are far too complicated for anyone outside the political class to comprehend—and anyone who succeeds in learning the inner workings of these systems inevitably winds up as a member of the political class.

exclusion.

Politics is the art of

segregation.

It is the specialization that lies at the root of all specialization and division of labor in this society: for if decisions regarding society as a whole can only be made through the proper channels, what use is it for anyone to concern himself with anything beyond his specific role? Once people accept their lot as peons in the belly of leviathan, they become significantly less interesting to each other.

Politics is the art of
REPRESENTATION

It presumes the inactivity of all but the political class. If everyone acted for herself, it would be pure anarchy—besides, people aren't used to thinking or acting for themselves nowadays, are they? Thus it happens that people only participate in the decisions that affect their lives from the sidelines, as spectators, cheering for one champion or another, and picking those champions as arbitrarily as one makes any inconsequential decision. In delegating their power, people give up the capacity to discover their desires: for one can only learn what one's interests are in the course of making decisions oneself. Some reformers hawk pipe dreams of more participatory systems of representation, but a world in which people act for themselves, directly, and thus need no representatives—that is unthinkable.

Politics is the art of
substitution.

The political representative stands in for all the power that the represented have given up. He becomes a prosthesis for their lost agency—they identify with him the way people watching a soap opera identify with the protagonists. The stronger he becomes at their expense, the stronger they feel.

Politics is the art of
01101101 01100101 01100100 01101001 01100001 01110100 01101001 01101111 01101110

Just as the Pope interprets the will of God, the scientist explains the edicts of Nature, and the professor passes on the lessons of History, the political professional mediates between people and their own power—with the consequence that they come to experience it as something alien and external. In representing people in the political arena, the politician becomes qualified to represent them to themselves: whatever he believes must be what they believe, whatever he does must be what they want, or else he wouldn't have ended up there. Likewise, when people relate to one another outside the strictly political realm, it is not as unique beings, but as roles within an established order. Between every person and every other, and between all persons and the structure of the society they comprise, there are filters that thwart all but a few standard forms of communication and interaction. As in organized religion, where there are no relationships between human beings but only between believers, so in politics it is not individuals who come together, but party members, activists, citizens.

Politics is the art of assimilation.

It teaches you to think in terms of majorities, to judge right and wrong according to public opinion rather than your own conscience. At best, the one thus educated must persuade himself and others that, although it may not appear to be the case, the vast majority of people want—or would want!—the same ends he does; at worst, and more often, this education leaves him feeling powerless in the face of society at large. In losing election after election and campaign after campaign, the one who seeks to sway the majority learns how small and ineffectual he is, how little he can accomplish—without ever hazarding the experiment of testing his own capabilities. If you can't beat them, join them, he inevitably concludes. Subsequently, the most unlikely coalitions form and struggle to outmaneuver one another in the race to gobble up enough constituents to form a majority.

Politics is the art of ABSTRACTION.

It thrives wherever a program supplants the needs and desires of specific human beings. In order that power can be delegated to the professionals that represent constituencies, the unique characteristics and interests of broad swaths of people are summarized in gross generalizations. Many rush to make abstractions of themselves—for the simpler the label, the more brute force can presumably be mustered behind it. Widely divergent desires are lumped together and reduced to their lowest common denominators in general platforms. Politicians represent people, and woe to those who refuse administration; abstractions represent demographics, and woe to those who defy classification!

Politics is the art of *Distraction*.

In a volatile society, it is a pressure valve, offering a constructive activity for those whose dissent might otherwise take destructive forms, so that their efforts to contest the status quo only serve to stabilize it. For the rebel, it is a wild goose chase that wastes all the energy and brilliant ideas she has to offer, confining her to dialogue with those she should be fighting and to fighting with those with whom she should be in dialogue.

Politics is the art of . . . deferme

Its solutions are always around the corner. As everyone knows, not least the politician, the problems we face can only be solved collectively—and we will do so, all together, but tomorrow, when everyone is ready. (I revolt, therefore we are—but if we are, farewell revolt.) In the meantime, each individual is asked to behave herself and wait, "just like everyone else"—in short, to give up all her strengths and opportunities, to paralyze herself voluntarily so she can be represented, with all that entails. In politics, the adventure of changing the world is transformed into the tedium of petitioning for it to change. Anyone who wants to act immediately, despite the drawbacks of the moment and the limitations inherent in any specific action, is always looked on with suspicion: if she is not an agent provocateur, the argument goes, her enemies can certainly use her as one.[†]

Politics is the art of calcula+ion.

In politics, one no longer has friends, but allies; one no longer has relationships, but associations; one's community becomes a pool from which to draw potential foot soldiers to be deployed and manipulated like chess pieces. It is necessary to know how things stand, to choose one's investments carefully, to weigh and measure every possibility—to assess every opportunity and categorize every individual and group, just as one's enemies do. In strategically appraising what one has, one gains everything but the readiness to lay it on the line and risk losing it.

Politics is the art of accommodation.

However radical the change one awaits, one must still survive somehow as one waits for the world to change, and in surviving—as we all know—one makes compromises. Sooner or later, the most intractable rebel must form some kind of alliance with the powers that be: I won't bother you if you don't bother me. Common sense, a perennial partisan of survival, can always come up with good reasons for making oneself agreeable: there are some compromises that are not so bad, it turns out, and is not the first duty of the revolutionary to live to fight another day? Always resigning oneself to settling for the lesser evil, little by little one accepts evil itself as acceptable. Anyone who contrarily wants to have nothing to do with evils at all must be an adventurist.

One of the most effective ways to divert desire for real change back into politics is to portray a political professional as subversive, or—better yet—to transform a subversive into a political professional. Not all politicians campaign for office; some even campaign **Politics is** against it, just as certain philosophers make a comfortable living decrying **the art of** the hands that feed them. Reality— they know this well, and this is all they **cooption.** know about it—is always more complex than any single action could address. They strive to develop a theory that accounts for the totality of social ills, so they will be totally absolved of the responsibility to do anything about them.

Politics is the art of

Once compromises have been made, once the social contract has been struck, tear gas and plastic bullets are no longer necessary to keep people in line. People will keep themselves in line, waiting at the movie theater, sitting in traffic on the way to work, paying their rent and taxes and obeying every rule and regulation—and if some starry-eyed rebels will not, then their own fellow radicals will see to it that they do, for nothing is more precious than the good name of radicalism. The moment someone does something rash, others hurry to deny that anyone of their persuasion would actually do such a thing, and to reeducate those from their own ranks who might furtively approve. Nothing is more terrifying than the specter of a single human being who will not play along with the collective madness—for if such a thing is possible for one person, what does that say about everyone else? Every unique, self-determined action is a spark that shoots beyond the confines of both the status quo and abstract critiques thereof, threatening both, not to mention those who uphold them.

Politics is the art of

Repression of anyone who does not accept the limitations of her social role, who wants to change things on the basis of her own desires. Repression of anyone who longs to be done with passivity, deliberation, and delegation. Repression of anyone who does not want to let her precious self be supplanted by any organization or immobilized by any program. Repression of anyone who wants to have unmediated relationships and recognizes that this means tearing down barriers, both social and physical. Repression of anyone who disrupts the precious compromises of those who wait patiently. Repression of anyone who gives herself without hope of compensation—of anyone who defends her companions with love and resoluteness—of anyone who refuses to accommodate herself to the consolation prizes offered to penitent rebels. Repression of anyone who neither wants to govern nor to control—of anyone who wants to live and act immediately, not tomorrow or the day after tomorrow—of anyone who wants to transform life into a joyous and daring adventure.

Politics is not an *Art* at all.

It is the opposite of art: the obliteration of creativity and spontaneity, the reduction of human relations to a network of interlocking chains. Likewise, any art which is to be worthy of the name—the art of living, for example—must be the opposite of politics: it must draw people together, give them access to their hidden strengths, enable them to do what they think is right without fearing what the neighbors will think or calculating what's in it for them.

† But only if she resolves "I myself, right here, right now!" can she then make a common cause with others that is not a space of mutual renunciation in which all are free to control one another but not to act for themselves. The dignity of acting for the sake of abiding by one's conscience, the joy that is sufficient unto itself without expectation that tomorrow will return interest on the investment: only these can carry us into a world in which our eyes will no longer be fixed constantly on the hands of the clock.

We owe our freedom to the spontaneous interplay
of myriad forces within and between us

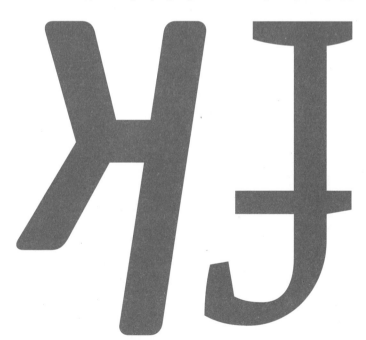

We chose the unfortunately named typeface **Tuna** for the text of this book on account of its excellent legibility at small sizes both in print and on screen, as well as the playful details at the edges of its low-contrast letterforms. Its rigor and modernity made it a perfect fit for the subject. Released in 2017, it was created in Germany by expert typographers Felix Braden and Alex Rütten.

The display font used throughout is TT Lakes (often in its **Condensed Bold** *Italic* variation), a simple and functional sans-serif with a beautiful italic that effortlessly conveys movement and direction. Chancing upon a historical railway station signplate in the Russian town of Priozersk (a Finnish town until WWII), Russian designer Ivan Gladkikh was inspired to create the typeface as an homage to Finnish functionalists Umlaut. It was released in 2016 in St. Petersberg.